the
father
of the
bride's
speech & duties

the father of the bride's speech & duties

hamlyn

confetti.co.uk

An Hachette UK Company
www.hachette.co.uk

First published in Great Britain in 2008 by
Hamlyn, a division of Octopus Publishing Group Ltd
Endeavour House
189 Shaftesbury Avenue
London
WC2H 8JY
www.octopusbooks.co.uk

ISBN: 978-0-600-61778-5

A CIP catalogue record for this book is available from the
British Library

Printed and bound in China

10 9 8 7 6 5 4 3

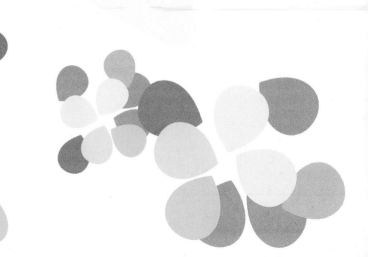

contents

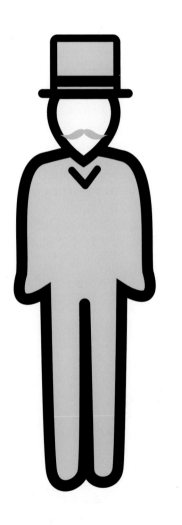

Introduction

Your daughter is getting married – congratulations! This is the day you have been waiting for and you will no doubt be feeling elated, proud and maybe even a little emotional now that it is finally happening. However, as these joyous feelings begin to fade, they may well be replaced by a sense of dread and even panic as you think about everything that needs to be done in preparation for the big day as well as all the things that might go wrong. If this is the case, don't worry; it's perfectly normal to have concerns and this book is here to help you.

Your daughter's wedding is likely to be one of the biggest events in your life. As father of the bride, it is only natural for you to want the best for your little girl and to want to be a father she can be proud of. Your role is to make sure everything goes smoothly for her both in the run up to, and on, the big day. You will have a number of 'official' duties to perform – giving your daughter away and making a great speech being the most important. Depending on the type of wedding, however, there may also be other ways in which you will be asked to help. Perhaps you will be consulted on choosing the right venue for the reception or be asked to help organize transport to and from the various locations. There will also doubtless be any number of occasions during the preparations when your calming influence and wise counsel are required, whether you are solving a thorny seating issue or lending a shoulder to cry on after a premarital tiff.

This practical book covers everything you need to know about how best to contribute to your daughter's wedding. It will be your indispensable guide in the run-up to the big day. Each chapter takes you through a key stage of your role in the wedding, offering plenty of tips and advice along the way.

The first chapter talks about the engagement – how you might react to the news and steps you should take in announcing the union formally. The following chapter discusses the intricacies of planning for the big day: budget issues, family matters and the question of what to wear. In the next chapter you will find a list of ways in which you can help out, from organizing cars, to making suggestions for venues to selecting the wine for the reception. This is followed by a chapter outlining your duties on the big day, and what will be expected of you. The final chapters guide you through the challenge of making a speech. Here you'll discover exactly what you should (and should not) include and how to deal with nerves. Finally, there is a great selection of sample speeches, jokes, one-liners and toasts to help you write and deliver the perfect speech with wit, warmth and confidence.

For more ideas and resources, why not visit our website (www.confetti.co.uk)? There you will find expert advice on your duties as father of the bride as well as more inspiring ideas for your speech.

Hearing
the
news

The proud father

Your precious little girl is getting married. Now is the time to reflect on this great step and your joint excitement as your daughter begins a new phase in her life.

Even if your daughter left home years ago, you may feel that this is the point at which she really becomes someone else's responsibility.

You probably know your daughter's fiancé well already, but make an extra effort now to welcome him into your family.

What might be expected of you
Here is a handy list of things you might be involved with:
- Expect to offer financial help. Weddings can be expensive and it is not unusual for the father of the bride to cover a number of the wedding costs.
- If you are paying for the wedding, you will probably also be responsible for deciding on the number of guests and for organizing the wedding invitations.
- The bride and groom might ask you to help decide on what the men in the wedding party should wear.
- You are likely to be responsible for arranging the transport to and from the various venues.
- You may help by finding and hiring a photographer.
- You could assist in choosing a venue and caterers for the reception.
- You may also be required to sort out entertainment for the reception.

Being a fab FOB

How much you get involved with the wedding planning is up to you, and the bride and groom of course. Some fathers choose to participate in all aspects of the wedding preparations, others prefer to allow the groom, the bride and her mother to make the arrangements. Apart from the formal aspects of your role you'll probably find yourself giving lots of support. Here are a few suggestions for things you can do.

Offer a helping hand

Do you know a lot about wine? Offer to taste the wine at the chosen venue. Know a little about photography? Perhaps you could help review the work of potential snappers. Or can you help by offering your garden as a convenient location for a marquee?

Look after the bride

Many brides take on too much of the wedding planning. Why not let your daughter delegate a few tasks to you? Offer to pick up chair covers, drop off cake samples or drive her to her dress fittings.

Be supportive

Nothing is likely to upset a bride more than if her parents seem uninterested in her wedding planning. Visit the venue and keep up to date with the ins and outs of ordering the dress. These little gestures are worth their weight in gold.

Always be there for your daughter. She might need a shoulder to cry on, or someone to vent frustration at. Let her know she can rely on you for a sympathetic ear.

Likely list of duties
As the father of the bride, you may not be particularly visible in the run-up to the wedding, but you've a very large and important role to play. You may well be:
- Paying for a large proportion of the wedding.
- Acting as host on the day.
- Making a speech.
- Giving your daughter away.

The good news

Gaining a son

It is traditional for the groom's parents to 'call on' the bride's parents soon after their children have decided to marry, but it doesn't always happen nowadays.

Generally, you will meet the groom's parents at some stage during the engagement, but these days there doesn't seem to be any hurry to make the introductions. It's a nice idea, though, to get together with your future in-laws as soon after the engagement announcement as possible.

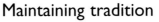

Maintaining tradition

In a recent poll, when asked the question, 'Should potential grooms ask permission from the bride's father?', 65 per cent of respondents answered 'yes'. It seems that the custom of seeking the permission of the father (or mother, or both) is alive and well.

If he asks you for permission

With many engagements taking place during romantic holidays abroad, your future son-in-law may ask you for permission over the phone rather than in person. Whether he's in the room or on the end of a long-distance line, keep it light, don't rib him too much and remember, it's probably taken a lot of guts for him to do this.

If he doesn't ask...

As more and more couples live together before marriage, and fewer brides are married from home, traditions such as asking permission to marry may no longer be appropriate, so don't feel offended if he doesn't ask you first. Remember he may well be doing this out of respect for your daughter. If he knows her well enough to marry her, he might also know that she is so independent that she would baulk at the thought of someone asking her father for her hand in marriage. Or maybe she proposed to him!

Meeting the in-laws

Once the engagement has been announced, it is traditional for the parents of the groom to write to the parents of the bride suggesting a date and venue for both families to meet. This is a particularly good idea if you have never met or do not know each other very well. It is a great chance for you to meet properly in a relaxed setting.

What should you offer your daughter?

Only you will know how much involvement your daughter is expecting from you. A young, first-time bride will almost certainly need some financial aid, and will probably welcome help with the planning. An older, financially independent daughter might only ask that you give her away. Use your judgement to assess the situation and be open with your daughter; make it clear from the beginning how much you would like (or are prepared) to be involved and make it easy for her to approach you. Above all, consider any suggestions that she might have regarding your role, even if they do not fit with your more conventional expectations.

Announcing the engagement formally

You'll be keen to tell as many relatives and friends as possible the good news of your daughter's engagement. Compile a list of those you want to contact and then check with your daughter whether she would like to tell them herself or if she is happy for you to tell them, whether by phone, letter, email or at a party.

It is traditional for the bride's parents to announce the news in the press. The usual wording is given in the examples below, but this can be easily altered to suit your personal circumstances.

Wording for a local newspaper
Mr and Mrs Robert Smith of Spring Cottage, Dover, Kent are delighted to announce the engagement of their daughter Anne Jane to Mark, son of Mr and Mrs Brian Shaw of Kingsbridge, Devon.

Wording for a national newspaper
The engagement is announced between Mark, younger son of Mr and Mrs Brian Shaw of Kingsbridge, Devon, and Anne Jane, only daughter of Mr and Mrs Robert Smith of Dover, Kent.

A good excuse for a get-together

If your daughter is still living at home, you might be required to host an engagement party. However, she may want to make a splash at a local bar, club or other hired venue, in which case you may not be involved any more than in contributing to the cost. If she chooses to host the party at her house or a house shared with her fiancé, you may not even be doing that.

A wedding is essentially a family occasion. To help this one go off without a hitch, this could be a good time for you to have a party on a smaller scale, one that just involves your immediate family. Perhaps there are close family members whom you have not seen for a while – an older sister who lives abroad or a son away at university. Perhaps there are family members whose relationships are strained. Whatever your circumstances, try to get all your relatives together around the time the engagement is announced. It does not have to be a formal event – you can meet at your home, in the pub or a local restaurant – but make sure that someone else takes care of the food so that you and your wife are free to host the party. A small intimate do is the ideal occasion to break the ice, heal old wounds and, above all, celebrate.

Been there, done that

If you are the father of a second-time bride, it may be difficult to be enthusiastic when you hear the news of your daughter's engagement, particularly if you feel that you gave your all the first time round. It could well be that you simply cannot face (or afford) the expense of a second wedding, or you may not want to be as involved in the planning as you were last time. Don't worry: the chances are that your daughter feels the same way.

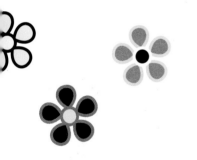

It is very unusual for a second-time bride to expect a great deal of involvement from her father when it comes to arranging the wedding. For starters, she is likely to be quite a bit older now, more financially independent and less family orientated. She might even have children, or be about to acquire some. A grand wedding is often deemed inappropriate second-time round and the couple are likely to prefer a less formal occasion, possibly just with very close family and friends. Second weddings tend not to be church weddings, and you are unlikely to be asked to give the bride away.

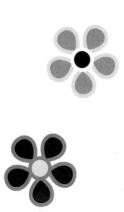

Even if your daughter *does* ask for advice and/or help, there are plenty of ways to make the occasion a special one, without it becoming a burden emotionally, financially or logistically:

- Suggest a very small, private church wedding to which only a handful of close friends or relatives are invited. You could offer your house as a venue for the reception.
- A couple with different faiths, or who had a church wedding first-time round and do not wish to do so again, could opt for an equally spiritual humanist wedding in a location that is very special to them as a couple.
- If the wedding is uniting two big families, a large-scale event may be impossible to avoid. In this instance, you could suggest hiring a wedding planner and offer to contribute to the cost.
- With families where the bride and groom have a number of mature siblings, you could appeal to them to help organize the wedding, each contributing to a different aspect of the arrangements, such as the transport, flowers or food.

Early
days

Money matters

Budgeting for the wedding

There's only one real rule when it comes to budgeting for your daughter's wedding: plan for the type of wedding you (or your daughter and future son-in-law) can realistically afford.

The average wedding costs somewhere in the region of £18,000. Around £1,500 of that is spent on the rings, £1,600 on the wedding outfits and essential pampering in the run-up to the big day, and £1,300 on the wedding itself. The reception costs around £4,500 and, finally, of course, there's the honeymoon and other expenses that vary from couple to couple.

Traditionally, it falls to you as the father of the bride to pick up the tab for the main event, with the groom paying for the church or register office fees and the honeymoon. As more and more couples now choose to pay for the bulk of their wedding themselves it's important to work out from the start who is paying for what and whether there are any financial constraints.

If you are contributing to, or paying for, the wedding, it's a good idea to clarify exactly how much say you want to have when it comes to organizing the event. You may have strong views on the venue, the food, the music, the cake or the order of the day and may feel it's only fair that you should play a part in the planning, rather than just being the one to pay the bills.

Often the groom's parents are pleased to contribute financially to the occasion in some way. However, you should not expect the groom's parents to share the bill.

If the groom's parents do make an offer and you are all happy for them to contribute, make a list of who's paying for what as soon as possible, to avoid any unpleasant misunderstandings. One common solution is for the groom's family to provide the wedding cake and pay for any food at the evening reception. Or they may want to do a straight 50:50 split with you, or a three-way split between you and your daughter and future son-in-law. Just make sure that you clarify from the start how the costs are likely to break down.

Splitting the cost of the wedding

The list below outlines who traditionally pays for what. Use it as a starting point to discuss who will do (and pay for) what.

The father of the bride pays for:
- The engagement and wedding press announcements
- The bride's and bridesmaids' dresses (although many brides now pay for their own dress)
- Flowers for the church and reception (except the bouquets and buttonholes)
- Photographer/videomaker
- Wedding stationery
- The reception and all that entails – the big expense

The groom pays for:
- The wedding rings
- All church/register office expenses
- The bride's bouquet, bridesmaids' flowers and buttonholes for the male members of the wedding party
- Transport
- Presents for the best man, ushers and bridesmaids
- The hotel on the first night
- The honeymoon

Budget advice

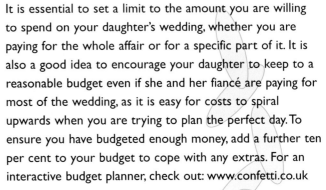

It is essential to set a limit to the amount you are willing to spend on your daughter's wedding, whether you are paying for the whole affair or for a specific part of it. It is also a good idea to encourage your daughter to keep to a reasonable budget even if she and her fiancé are paying for most of the wedding, as it is easy for costs to spiral upwards when you are trying to plan the perfect day. To ensure you have budgeted enough money, add a further ten per cent to your budget to cope with any extras. For an interactive budget planner, check out: www.confetti.co.uk

Open a wedding account
It is a good idea to open a wedding account and pay in a regular sum each month, preferably by standing order or direct debit. All bills can be paid from this account and it is easy to keep track of how much is being spent.

Shop around
The easiest way to save money is not to pay over the odds. Ask for quotations in writing and make sure you know exactly what the price agreed covers. Remember that you may need to add VAT to some prices, so always ask.

Take out insurance
Wedding insurance will cover eventualities such as damage to the dress, cancellation of the reception due to illness and double booking of the venue. However, it won't pay out if the bride or groom get cold feet on the big day!

Bright ideas

There are many ways in which you can keep down the cost of a wedding. If there are budget constraints then consider some of the following:

- Hold the wedding on a weekday, when venues may charge less.
- Check if you can supply your own wine for the reception. For the toasts, opt for an inexpensive sparkling wine rather than champagne, then have a pay bar for the rest of the evening.
- Rather than your daughter buying a new wedding dress, hire one, have one made or buy or hire a worn-once dress.
- Ask your wife or her friends to do the church flowers in order to save on florist's costs. Seasonal flowers will be cheaper.
- Use a good photographer, but preferably one whose company is small enough not to charge VAT. Or ask your arty friends to take the wedding photos.
- Make use of friends with posh cars to transport the wedding party to the church or venue.
- Invite more casual friends to an evening drink rather than the full wedding with all its catering costs.
- Ask a relative or friend with culinary talents to make the cake as their wedding gift.
- Forego the professional DJ and get the engaged couple to use their own CDs.
- Suggest the couple leave for their honeymoon on a weekday.
- Propose that the guests give honeymoon vouchers rather than presents.

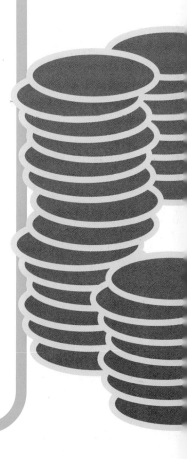

A very personal touch

Every wedding is different

Not all weddings are conventional, and it is increasingly the case these days that the bride and groom plan their wedding between themselves, with relatively little help from family and friends. Your daughter may be getting married for the second time or be in a position, with her partner, to cover the cost of her own wedding. Either way, all she may want from you is a blessing and your presence on the day.

But will this be enough for you? It is easy to feel rejected if your daughter does not want the full father-of-the-bride treatment. After all, you have 25 years' worth of great speech material. Not only that, but what if you want to make a special contribution as a way of expressing your love for your daughter and your acceptance of her fiancé? If you are not contributing to the wedding financially, or personally taking care of a number of arrangements, it is difficult to influence your daughter's wedding plans without being seen as interfering or trying to run the show.

Making a special contribution

If your daughter really does not want your help, here are some other ways in which you can make your own personal contribution:

- A fortnight before the wedding, invite your daughter, her fiancé and his parents to join you and your wife at a top restaurant to mark the start of the celebrations, and to share one last intimate meal together before the wedding.
- A week before the wedding, send your daughter a bunch of flowers, a bottle of champagne and a box of chocolates. Write a card to tell her how proud you are of her, and that you wish her well on the big day.
- Arrange for a luxury food hamper or a case of champagne to be delivered to the happy couple's home on their return from honeymoon.
- Make a substantial cash donation towards a new home, a new car or other domestic venture.
- Plant a tree to celebrate their wedding day.
- Offer to make an annual donation to a charity of their choice on their behalf.
- Send your daughter a bunch of flowers every month for the first year of her marriage.
- Set up and contribute towards a savings account for their future – for their children or a home abroad, for example.

The guest list

Working out the guest list

Deciding on the guest list is usually when the wedding party comes to blows, so as father of the bride this is a crucial time to use your tact and diplomacy. While traditionally as hosts of the wedding you and your wife will send out the invitations, the bride and groom should have the chance to each invite a similar number of guests. One way to do this is to split the list into three – one third for the bride's family, one third for the groom's family and one third for the couple's friends.

Start by asking everyone involved to make a rough list of guests, then start pruning. Ultimately, if you are paying for the wedding then you should have the final say on numbers, and naturally if your daughter and her fiancé are paying then they will decide on numbers. Usually it works out that the hosts and the couple decide together who goes on the list.

You should add the names of the minister and his or her partner to your list as a matter of courtesy, and when it comes to working out numbers, make sure you include all members of the wedding party – people sometimes forget to include themselves!

If you have relatives who you know won't be able to make it on the day, obviously you don't need to include them on the guest list, but make sure they are sent an invitation. Many people, in particular elderly relatives, really appreciate this gesture – it shows that you haven't just forgotten or ignored them.

Keeping numbers down

If the wedding venue is too small to invite everyone to for the ceremony, ask them to celebrate with you after the marriage at the reception. No one should take offence at this arrangement. It's not a cheap solution, though, and the major factor for limiting numbers may well be cost rather than space.

If money is more of an issue than space, you can limit the number of guests you invite to the wedding breakfast to close family and friends, and then ask everyone else to come to the evening celebrations, if that is an option.

Not inviting children will also help to reduce numbers, but make sure that all the parents know well in advance (see page 43).

Playing the diplomat

Worried that relatives may be offended if they are not invited? Option one, which is not advised, is to demand they are included. Option two is to take some of the burden off your daughter by phoning the relatives, explaining that numbers are limited and arranging to visit them afterwards with the video, or to send them copies of the photos.

Many venues nowadays are not suitable for children, either in size or facilities, and your daughter may decide she wants a child-free wedding. This is often a difficult decision to make, so offer to phone relatives with children to explain the situation.

Family matters

Keeping everyone happy

Nothing brings a girl and her mother closer than planning for a wedding. But, at the same time, it may offer plenty of potential for friction. Keep an eye out for building storms. Often it only takes a sympathetic phone call or a comforting cup of tea to get things back to normal between your daughter and your wife.

Some lucky families seem to be blessed with sisters who are the best of friends, but if the relationship is not so perfect you should be prepared for cracks to emerge during the planning period. If the relationship between your daughters erupts, be on hand to lend an ear, but stay impartial. Taking sides is never a good idea.

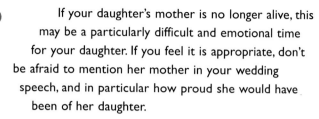

If your daughter's mother is no longer alive, this may be a particularly difficult and emotional time for your daughter. If you feel it is appropriate, don't be afraid to mention her mother in your wedding speech, and in particular how proud she would have been of her daughter.

If you have remarried, your daughter may want to involve her stepmother but may fear it will upset her mother. By all means, come up with suggestions for including her stepmother, but accept that it just may not be possible. If you think your current wife is not playing a large enough role, remember the bride is busy making compromises and trying to please as many people as possible.

Finally, there is one potential area of dispute that it is best to avoid. If your wife is not seeing eye to eye with the groom's mother, resist any temptation to get involved or take sides. Remember, you may both be grandparents to the same children one day! If possible, try and offer some solutions to the sticking points.

Keeping all your children happy

Some brides are put under pressure from their parents to choose their nieces or nephews as bridesmaids or page-boys. If you're blessed with angelic grandchildren, then of course you'd love to see them play a part in your daughter's special day. But if she's not keen, don't push it. After all, if they're that cute, they'll surely be snapped up by another bride!

Dad number two

Brides with two fathers can face a number of wedding day dilemmas, from the wording on the invitations to who should give the father-of-the-bride speech. Bear in mind that this is your daughter's day and it is your role to make it as stress-free as possible. Both you and her stepfather can play an important part on the big day, so – regardless of any feelings or history between you – remember that the father of the bride role is big enough for *both* of you.

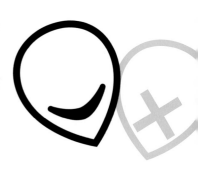

The invitations

In a family with two fathers, invitations can be an especially sensitive issue. If one set of parents wants to host, then this can leave the others feeling left out.

One way round the issue is to put both families on the invitation (even if it is a bit lengthy). The wording then might be: 'Mr… (*bride's father*) and his family, and Mrs… (*bride's mother*) and her family, would like to invite you to their daughter's wedding to…'

Giving away

Although traditionally you should walk your daughter down the aisle, for various reasons she might want her stepfather rather than you. If this is the case try not to feel put out. This is far from the only way you can play a part in your daughter's wedding. She knows this too, so why not get your heads together and plan a role just for you.

Speech sensitivities

What should you do if your daughter wants to involve
both you and her stepfather in the speeches – who makes
the father-of-the-bride speech?

Perhaps you could give the father-of-the bride speech
and her stepfather could compere all the speeches,
introducing each speaker and explaining their relationship
to the bride and groom. Or maybe both of you could make
speeches covering different aspects of her life.

The top table

The bride might want both her father and stepfather at the
traditional top table, but worry that some people might
think it strange.

As it is your daughter's big day it is best to follow her
wishes. Either reorganize the traditional top table to allow
for extended family, or don't have a top table and follow a
different seating plan (see page 78).

Two mums, too?

While some daughters are more than happy to involve
their stepmother in the proceedings, others worry about
upsetting their natural mothers or simply do not get on
with their stepmother. If your current wife is likely to feel
left out, get together with your daughter to find ways of
making your wife more comfortable on the day.

- Arrange for her to sit with close friends at the reception
  if she is not included on the top table.
- Put her in charge of any grandchildren.
- Arrange for one of the ushers to keep an eye on her.

What are you wearing?

The correct attire

Traditionally, the father of the bride, the best man, ushers and page-boys all take their lead from the outfit chosen by the groom, and it is up to the groom or best man to select the outfits. It is worth remembering though that the bride usually has strong preferences on what she wants the men in the wedding party to wear.

You should expect to be consulted on what the male members of the wedding party are going to wear, but basically you should follow the groom's lead unless there is a particular reason not to, for example you want to wear your family tartan.

If suits are being hired, for consistency it is best for everyone to have their fittings done together or at least use the same supplier. Remember that a hired suit needs to be fitted and ordered well in advance. It is usual for each person to pay for his own hire cost.

Even if you are dressed like the rest of the men in the wedding party, you might still want to look a little different. Do this by wearing a different colour waistcoat, special buttonhole or fancy cravat. Don't spring any wild colour or pattern surprises on your daughter, though!

Wedding style

There are many different styles of wedding attire. Below are some of the most popular options.

Morning dress

The morning suit (penguin suit, top hat and tails) is usually worn for weddings before 3pm, and is still the most popular attire. The cut and style of the coat is very flattering to the majority of figures, and consists of a blue or black tailcoat (only the groom may wear a grey tailcoat) paired with matching or contrasting trousers, either plain or pinstriped. The outfit is completed by a white wing-collar shirt, a waistcoat of any colour, a cravat, a top hat and gloves (just held, not worn).

Black tie

Black tie is traditionally worn for weddings later in the day and is ideal for a grand evening reception or summer ball. A black dinner jacket, single- or double-breasted, with ribbed silk lapels and no vents or covered buttons is worn. Trousers should be tapered, suitable for braces and have one row of braid. The evening shirt, in cotton or silk, with either a marcella or a pleated front, has a soft, turn-down collar. White tie is not usually worn at weddings.

Accessories

Cummerbunds may be worn (with pleats opening upwards), but waistcoats are more acceptable. The bow tie is of black silk, but black tie can also be individualized with a colourful bow tie, matching waistcoat and pocket handkerchief. Shoes should be black and well polished, and socks plain black.

What are you wearing?

Lounge suit

The important thing at any event, and especially at a wedding, is to feel at ease. Lounge suits are a good alternative to more formal attire. This is definitely a sharp and sophisticated choice, and while associated with register office weddings, is perfectly acceptable for religious weddings as well.

Got the blues?

If you are a member of the armed forces (or you are retired from the armed forces), then it is acceptable for you to wear your regimental uniform. The traditional uniform for weddings is the 'Blues' uniform: a blue jacket with a high collar, adorned with five brass buttons down the front and two on each cuff for officers. The jacket is teamed with matching blue trousers with a red stripe down the outside of each leg. No shirt is worn but the uniform is accessorized with a white belt and gloves.

Traditional outfit

The best-known and most popular of these is Highland morning or evening dress, traditionally worn by Scottish grooms. The kilt should be accompanied by a Bonnie Prince Charlie jacket or doublet, a sporran, laced brogues, socks, bow tie and *sgian-dhu* (a small dagger carried in your sock).

Beach wedding

If the wedding is going to be on a beach or in a hot climate, there's a whole range of options available. In the linen suit department there's everything from Man from Del Monte/Pierce Brosnan chic to *Miami Vice* crushed casual style. Just remember: light shirts, no ties, Panama hats optional. Or how about a custom-made silk suit?

Overseas advice

If you want to smarten up your act a bit, a white tuxedo is great for overseas weddings in hot climates. A white jacket is best teamed with black trousers, a white pleated-front evening shirt and a black bow tie.

Shoes

The choice of shoes is also personal, although the rule is not to wear brown shoes with black trousers and vice versa. A well-fitting pair of leather shoes is your best choice.

Finishing touches

How to tie a tie
The following are simple instructions for three classic tie styles.

The Bow Tie
1 Start with A 4 cm (1½ in) below B.
2 Take A over then under B.
3 Double B in half and place across the collar points.
4 Hold B with thumb and index finger; drop A over.
5 Pull A through a little, then double A and pass behind, then through the hole in front.
6 Poke resulting loop through; even the tie out and then tighten.

The Four-in-Hand
1 Start with A about 50 cm (20 in) below B.
2 Take A behind B.
3 Continue wrapping right round.
4 Pull A up through the loop.
5 Pull A down through loop in front.
6 Tighten.

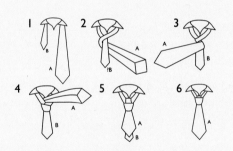

The Windsor
1 Start with A about 60 cm (24 in) below B.
2 Take A behind B and up through loop.
3 Bring A over and behind B.
4 Take A down through loop again.
5 Then over and up through loop.
6 Bring through the knot and tighten.

Top tips for looking good

1 Get measured properly – especially if you suspect your waist measurement may have expanded. Admitting you're no longer a size 34 could save you from having to spend the whole wedding day holding your breath in case you pop a button.

2 Accessorize! Think smart cufflinks, shirt studs, a decent watch (not the one you got free at the garage), a tie pin, bow tie, buttonhole, braces, a cummerbund, waistcoat, handkerchief – and, of course, your shoes, which need to be in keeping with the whole outfit.

3 So well groomed you're often mistaken for Roger Moore? Or do people have difficulty telling you and Bob Geldof apart? Either way, this really is a day for looking your best. And that means a haircut, a good shave and even a manicure. Go on, you might enjoy it!

4 Check your outfit two weeks before the wedding day in case you've lost weight, collected the wrong size shirt or there's been a bad attack of moths.

5 Wedding photographs are a long-lasting souvenir of the big day. Just remember: don't slouch and look happy.

How you
might help

Organizing and sending the invitations

Ideally, invitations should be ordered at least three months before the wedding and as soon as you have an idea of the number of people attending.

Allow one invitation per family, including a courtesy one for the groom's parents and the minister and his wife or her husband. Also include family and friends whom you may already know cannot come, but who would appreciate receiving an invitation anyway.

Don't forget to order a spare 20 or so invitations to allow for mistakes when writing them and for any extra guests who are asked at a later date.

The invitations should be sent out at least six weeks before the wedding to allow as much time for organization as possible. Between 10 and 12 weeks before the wedding is the average length of time.

Invitation style
The wedding stationery can include anything from a simple card invitation to a complete wedding pack – it all depends on personal preference and the style of the wedding.

Reception invitations

If you are sending out invitations for the wedding reception or evening reception only, these can take the same form as any usual party invitation.

Designing the invitations

Invitations can set the style for the wedding, whether traditional or out of the ordinary. Designs to suit all tastes and budgets are available from good stationers and local printers, or buy card and create your own.

How you break up the lines on the invitation is a personal choice. Generally speaking, however, names, times and places are placed on separate lines. Bear in mind that fairly equal line lengths usually look better on the page than an array of different ones.

Different kinds of invitations

The classic wedding invitation is simply type (no graphics), ideally engraved on good-quality white or cream card. The format is an upright, folded card with the wording on one side. Black or silver lettering is the most popular.

Ready-printed cards are available where you fill in the details by hand, or you can create your own design and have a set of invitations printed or even create each invitation individually. If you select a traditional specially printed or engraved card, the guest's name is handwritten at the top left-hand side of the card.

Invitation traditions

Formal invitations

If you want to follow the traditional invitation style, there are several basic rules to follow:

- Invitations always go out from whoever is hosting the wedding, which is normally you and your wife.
- Invitations are generally written in the third person, such as Mr & Mrs Jones, rather than 'we'.
- When listing the time, date and venue on the invitation, the time and date should be written first, the venue last.
- Use titles, for example Mrs, Dr, Sir, when appropriate. There is no need for a full stop after Mr, Mrs or Dr.
- 'The honour of your presence' or 'the pleasure of your company' is the normal choice of wording. The former is often used for invitations to religious ceremonies, such as a church wedding, while the latter is preferred for invitations to an event in a non-religious location.
- The bride's name should appear before the groom's.

Other useful things to mention

It's also a good idea to include relevant information, for example:

- any dress requirements, such as black tie or smart dress
- whether any food will be served (if it's not a dinner/lunch party)
- when the reception will finish
- whether drinks are free for the entire reception.

Alternative wording

If you have been widowed:

Mr James Jones requests the pleasure…

If you have been divorced and your ex-wife has not remarried:

Mr James Jones and Mrs Pamela Jones request the pleasure…

If you have been divorced and your ex-wife has remarried:

Mr James Jones and Mrs Pamela Matthews request the pleasure…

If your daughter and her fiancé are hosting their own wedding:

Ms Mary Alice Jones and Mr Carl David Spencer request the pleasure of your company at their marriage, etc.

Inviting children

On the invitations, make it quite clear to parents that their children are invited by including their names and let them know up front if you have made special arrangements for them, such as: 'We have arranged child-minding facilities for the duration of the service and/or reception.'

There are two ways of letting people know that children are not invited. The first is to tell parents tactfully before the invitations go out. The second way is to enclose a short note to parents, clearly but tactfully saying something like: 'We are sorry that we are unable to invite babies and children to the wedding.' Printing 'no children' on the invitations is not an option.

Other stationery

There is a significant amount of literature that, as father of the bride, you may be expected to produce. Some of it may be organized by your daughter or future son-in-law.

Response cards

Many people word their invitations to include an address to which guests can reply, but the best way of ensuring a quick reply is to send a response card with the invitation, which can be completed and returned to you.

Alternatively, buy a set of ready-printed RSVP cards – simple ones that won't clash with your invitation design.

It's a good idea to add a date, one or two months before the event, by when you would like the replies. After this date, ring round any stragglers for their answers.

Map and directions

The more detailed and carefully written the directions, the better. The map can be drawn by hand, photocopied or printed from a map website. You may also like to include details of the nearest train, tube or bus stations, as well as the numbers of local cab firms.

Local accommodation

For those travelling some distance, you can include a list of local hostels, B&Bs and hotels. Many hotels will allow block reservations of rooms, as long as they are confirmed by a certain date. This usually allows you to negotiate a more favourable rate, especially during the off-peak season.

Order of service

If your daughter is having a church wedding, the sample template below should help you to set out the order of service. Make sure that you check the content with whoever is conducting the service before having these printed.

Wedding gift list

Traditionally, the wedding gift list isn't included with the invitation; guests who wish to buy the bride and groom a present will ask you or your wife for details about the gift list. However, nowadays it's more acceptable to include the gift list with the invitation.

If circumstances change

Hopefully there will be no reason to postpone or cancel the wedding, but if it is necessary to do so, you need to let all the guests know formally. The usual wording is given below.

For postponements

Owing to the recent illness of Mrs Jones, the wedding of her daughter Susan to Mr Neil Wood at St Mary's Church at 2pm on Saturday 5th April, 2008 has been postponed to 3pm on Saturday 9th August, 2008.

For cancellations

Owing to the sudden death of Mrs Jones, the wedding of her daughter Susan to Mr Neil Wood will not now take place at St Mary's Church at 2pm on Saturday 5th April, 2008. The marriage will take place privately at a date to be decided.

Order of service
Front page
- Church and location
- The marriage of bride and groom
- Date and time

Inside pages
- Entrance music (processional) for bride
- Introduction
- Hymn (include words)
- The marriage
- Prayers (optional)
- Reading (optional)
- Blessing (optional)
- Hymn (include words)
- Reading/blessing (optional)
- Hymn (optional – include words)
- Signing of the register
- Exit music (recessional)

Arranging transport

Organizing the wedding cars

It is usual for the father of the bride to arrange the transport for the wedding day. Make sure that you discuss the arrangements fully with your daughter and future son-in-law as they may have strong preferences as to how they wish to arrive at —and leave — the church.

Remember, not all brides opt for the conventional way of travelling to the ceremony by car. If that's the case, you may be able to help organize whatever mode of transport your daughter has chosen. However, if she is going by car, you should consider how many cars will be needed, what colours or makes you all prefer, and what decorations you would like. An average order would be two cars from your home to the ceremony venue and three from there to the reception — the third car being for the newlyweds. Once you have worked out exactly what you want get quotes from a number of reputable firms and make the booking well in advance.

Crucially, it's your job to get the bride to the venue and in one piece. Keep the number of a taxi company on you in case of emergency, as well as maps to the venues, and if you don't have a mobile phone, borrow one. Just make sure it's switched off during the ceremony.

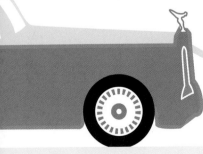

Travelling in style

Although a vintage Rolls Royce or Daimler is the traditional and certainly the most glamorous way to arrive at a wedding, there are some weird and wonderful alternatives that you could use:

- Classy motor – A stretch limousine adds a dash of Hollywood glamour to the proceedings. Alternatively, consider a classic American car such as a 1950s Cadillac. If the bride and groom are sports car fanatics, consider hiring a spectacular set of wheels and roll up in a racy Ferrari, Porsche or Aston Martin.
- Cabbing it – A white hackney cab is an inexpensive, practical and very stylish way to reach the wedding.
- Pony (and trap) – Make the perfect fairy-tale wedding with a horse and carriage. Intensely romantic and very picturesque, this mode of transport is perfect for a country wedding where there are no busy roads.
- Chopper's away – For an entrance worthy of a Bond girl, arrival by helicopter is not only a thrilling way to travel, but it can also be very practical, especially if the venue of the ceremony is some way from your home or the reception.
- Water berth – For a wedding in a riverside hotel, you and the bride could arrive by boat.
- Something on the side – For a cute and quirky means of transport to the ceremony, a vintage motorbike and sidecar would be perfect.

Arranging the photographer

Finding the right photographer

Whether you or your daughter are arranging the photographer, start the search early because good ones get booked up a long time in advance. Try to visit at least three photographers and check out their studio and staff before you make your final choice, and don't be afraid to ask questions. Ask to see full wedding album samples and make sure that the photos you're shown are the work of the person who will be taking the wedding pictures, not simply the best photos from the studio.

It is important to check credentials. See if the photographer is a qualified member of MPA (Master Photographers Association), BIPP (British Institute of Professional Photographers) or Guild of Wedding Photographers.

Whoever is booked to take the wedding pictures will be spending a substantial amount of time with you all on the big day. You must all get on with the photographer and feel confident and relaxed in his or her presence. If you don't, it will be reflected in the final images.

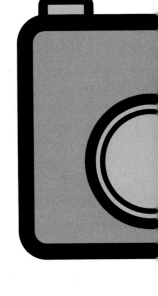

Is the price right?

Prices range from anything upwards of £500, and wedding photography is one area where you really do get what you pay for. Most photographers have a menu of prices and will charge a flat rate for taking shots on the day, plus an additional charge based on how many photographs the bride and groom want in their album as well as extra for any copies that you or other family members or friends want.

The quality of the albums on offer (leather, plastic, velvet) can vary enormously and this will affect the cost as well. Look out for those nice little extras – some photographers include handy thank-you cards with a small photo as part of the deal.

Photography checklist
- Once you or your daughter have decided on a style and photographer, ask the photographer to confirm the booking in writing.
- Check the small print and make sure you know exactly what you're getting for your money.
- Ask the photographer to sign a contract that records the wedding date, time and place, price and any restrictions or conditions.
- Ascertain when the proofs will be ready and how long the bride and groom can keep them in order to make their selection.
- Find out exactly when the album will be ready.

Briefing the photographer

Think style and colour

There are lots of different styles that photographers use to record weddings, from the formal and traditional posed group images to more candid and relaxed reportage-style shots, such as the bride in her curlers. Most couples choose a combination of styles and film.

Some photographers will shoot in both black-and-white and colour, while others will stick to one medium. Black-and-white creates a timeless image, but if the day has been carefully colour-coordinated then you will want colour photos that record this. If a lot of time has been spent creating invitations, menus, flower arrangements and the like, then you will want a photographer who will capture these little details on film, too.

For relaxed, unposed shots it is a good idea to place disposable cameras on the tables at the reception for guests to take their own pictures of the celebrations. Ask guests to leave the cameras behind at the end of the evening so that you or the bride and groom can develop the films. The photos will give a unique insight into the wedding day from other people's points of view.

Planning for the perfect pictures

Ask the photographer to check out the venues for the service and the reception before the big day, so that he or she can get a feel for the best settings to enhance the style of photographs. Remember to check with the minister to make sure photography is permitted during the wedding ceremony.

A good photographer will use his or her creative and technical skills to get great results, but make sure it's clear what role he or she should take. Should the photographer control events or blend into the background, focus on the people or pick up all the little details as well? One well-known photographer likes to shepherd guests into position with the help of a shrill whistle. It's not very subtle, but it breaks the ice and no one misses out on the photo calls.

Looking good

If you are not used to posing, practise before the wedding to find a smile or expression you can live with. If you look and feel comfortable, the photos are bound to work. Remember to stand up straight, with your head back, no double chins, and smile – you want to look your best!

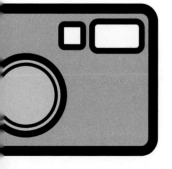

The shoot list

Before the big day, make sure the photographer has a rough shoot list. The traditional choices include:

- Groom and best man outside the church/civil venue
- Bride and her father's arrival at the church/civil venue
- Bride and her father walking down the aisle/bride entering the civil venue
- Bride and groom at the altar/desk
- Exchange of rings
- Signing of the church register/documentation
- Procession out of the church/civil venue
- Group shots outside the church/civil venue and reception
- Arriving at the reception
- Cutting the cake

Recording the wedding on video

Using a professional

For a slick and infinitely watchable video, you generally need to hire a professional videomaker. However, be warned: the cost can be prohibitive. The best way to find a videomaker is through recommendation. Alternatively, contact the Association of Professional Videomakers. Always ask to see samples of their work and watch a video of a whole wedding, not a tape of edited highlights. Make sure the same person who filmed the wedding you are watching will film your daughter's wedding.

Book the videomaker well in advance. Next determine exactly what is included in the price and whether there will be extra charges for editing, adding titles and dubbing music, and whether the bride and groom can choose their own music. Let the videomaker know if there are specific moments or people you want included in the video.

Using an amateur

If the budget won't stretch to hiring a professional, ask a friend or relative to video the wedding day. An amateur video will never be as perfect as a professionally made one, but it can still capture all the joy of the day.

Get your appointed 'cameraman' to experiment with the camera well in advance and plan what is to be filmed. Make sure a tripod is used for the ceremony as the footage will be steadier, and ensure that rapid zooming in or out is avoided, or the images will be blurred. Remember, too much footage is better than too little – the video can always be edited.

Photography and video checklist
Use the following checklist to help you clarify your
photography and/or video needs:
- Is the photographer/videomaker available before and after
  the ceremony and at the reception?
- How do they charge? Flat fee? By the hour?
- What kind of packages do they offer? Can substitutions
  be made?
- Are prints/extra videotapes included in the price? Is the
  cost of an album included in the price?
- Are they willing to follow a list of requested shots?
- Will they have an assistant/assistants? Is their cost
  included in the price?
- What will everyone be wearing?
- Are you expected to provide food and/or transportation?
- If there is an emergency, will you be sent an alternative
  photographer/videomaker? If yes, can you see examples of
  their work?
- How soon after the wedding will the proofs/tapes be
  available? How long can the bride and groom keep the
  proofs before making their selection?
- How long will the photographer keep the negatives?
- Who owns the rights to the images?
- How far in advance are bookings required?
- What is their policy on cancellation/postponement?
- How much is the deposit to secure the date?
- When is the deposit due?
- How soon after the event is the balance due?
- Is VAT included in the final price?
- Make sure all dates, times and locations are confirmed
  with a written contract.
- Get insurance.

Selecting a venue

Helping to choose a venue

You may have been asked to help choose a venue for the reception, and this can be quite a delicate matter. It is important for you to discuss all the options with your daughter and her fiancé before making any arrangements. Find out what they have in mind and do not try to impose your own view. This is likely to be the single biggest expense of the wedding so you will want to get it right – especially if you are paying.

Practical considerations when choosing a venue include the time of the wedding – will you need a venue that can accommodate a wedding breakfast for a morning ceremony or evening entertainment if the wedding is later in the day? You will also need to think about how people get to the reception venue and, more importantly, how they will get home when the wedding is over. If you are going for something a little less conventional, make sure the venue can cater for everything you need – electricity, lavatory and cloakroom facilities, adequate parking – or that alternative arrangements can be made.

Obvious choices of venue include hotels, clubs, the village hall or a stately home. Basic costs will cover the venue hire and food and drink, but many venues can also take care of the registrar, flower arrangements, a toastmaster and even accommodation. Get a full list of possible charges right at the beginning and select options that work with your budget.

Offering your home

Traditionally, the father of the bride will offer his home as a venue for the reception. This is a great option for a small, intimate family do, but harder to pull off for larger parties – say over 40 guests – unless you have a very large house. Having said this, if you have a garden of a reasonable size and hire a marquee then you can easily accommodate greater numbers, particularly if the marquee hire includes lavatory and cloakroom facilities. Either option gives you greater flexibility over refreshments and entertainment and often works favourably financially.

Ideas for a unique reception location
If your daughter cannot face another function at the golf club, here are some ideas for a less conventional venue:

- A museum or historic building: London's Natural History Museum and others cater for wedding receptions, as do plenty of landmark buildings from the Pump House in Bath to London's Tower Bridge. Some of them also have a civil wedding licence.
- Something different: a barn, a lighthouse, a racecourse, even the London Eye. There are countless less-conventional venues available year-round.
- For a wedding with a theme (it takes all sorts!) you could consider hiring a boat, a castle, even a zoo.

Hiring a marquee

A marquee is a good option for large gatherings. Even if your own garden isn't large enough or isn't appropriate for a marquee, you may have willing relatives or friends with a more suitable site.

Marquees are no longer simply poled tents. Nowadays, they are framed structures that don't need ropes or poles, and the space within the marquee is clear. Marquees come in a huge array of shapes, sizes, prices and specifications. Shop around and find out what is available. Remember that the marquee will need flooring and a lining as well as other components that are costed separately, for example lighting, heating and furniture – so you'll need to take these costs into consideration. Ask to see samples of fabrics used for the marquee lining – the wide choice of linings available means that you can choose colours that will complement the wedding theme. Because heated marquees are now available everybody should be cosy, whatever the weather.

Before booking the marquee it is a good idea to show the hire company the site to ensure that it's suitable for your requirements.

Marquee checklist

Consider the following before confirming the booking:

- Is the location close enough to the ceremony venue?
- Will holding the reception at home increase the stress factor dramatically?
- Are lavatory and cloakroom facilities sufficient or can the hire company arrange for portable toilets if necessary?
- Is there room for caterers in the kitchen of your home or will you need to hire a portable kitchen?
- Is there space for a bar?
- Is there sufficient parking space?
- Will the company do an on-site estimate?
- Will a marquee hold all the guests and a dance floor?
- What colour is the marquee? What linings are there?
- Are proper flooring and staging available?
- Is the hire of tables and chairs included in the price?
- Is there a sufficient power supply or can the hire company provide a generator?
- Can they provide interior lighting? Exterior lighting? Heating? A public address system for speeches?
- Is access to a permanent shelter/house available?
- Can walkways be covered?
- When will the marquee need to be set up and dismantled?
- Will someone be available at the event in an emergency?
- How far in advance are bookings required?
- What is the policy on cancellation/postponement?
- What is the deposit to secure the date? When is it due?
- How soon after the event is the balance due?
- Is VAT included in the final price?
- Confirm dates, times and details with a written contract.
- Get insurance.

Booking a venue

If your home isn't suitable for hosting your daughter's wedding, or she would simply like the wedding to be held somewhere else, make sure she has considered the following checklist before booking her chosen location. Also establish early on whether or not the management of the chosen venue is on your side – there are certain museums and historic buildings whose managers/caretakers would prefer to see their venues full of art or exhibits instead of wine and music.

Venue checklist

Make sure you have considered the following before confirming your booking:

- Is the venue big enough to accommodate all the guests?
- Is the venue close enough to the ceremony venue?
- Are there adequate parking facilities?
- Is there accommodation at the venue?
- What types of wedding package are available?
- Does the venue have an in-house wedding coordinator?
- Are there any special conditions imposed by the venue?
- Are there adequate cloakroom and lavatory facilities?
- Are there facilities and special seating for less mobile guests or anyone with a disability?
- Are there any special facilities for children?
- Is there equipment you can use? Will you have to hire tables, chairs, linen, crockery, cutlery, glassware?
- Are the tables, chairs, linen and overall ambience appropriate for the style of wedding?

- Are decorations, such as flowers, included?
- Can you bring in your own choice of caterer, florist, decorator and other services?
- If bringing in a caterer, will they have access to a kitchen, power supply and running water?
- Can the venue supply the cake stand and knife?
- Does the venue have a licence to consume alcohol? Is there a late-night curfew? When will the bar close?
- Can you supply your own alcohol? Is there a corkage fee?
- How will the staff be dressed? How many will be needed?
- Is a toastmaster included in the staffing costs?
- Is entertainment permitted?
- Is there a sufficient power supply for a sound system?
- Is there a public address system for speeches?
- Are there noise level restrictions?
- Where can guests store coats and personal belongings?
- Is there a safe place for storing gifts?
- Are there other weddings booked for the same day?
- When will you be allowed access to the venue?
- Is there a private room in which the bride and groom can change into their going-away outfits?
- Can you see the room while it's being used for another wedding reception?
- Does the venue have public liability insurance?
- How far in advance are bookings required?
- What is the policy on cancellation/postponement?
- How much is the deposit and when is it due?
- How soon after the event is the balance due?
- Is VAT included in the final price?
- Confirm dates, times and details with a written contract.
- Get insurance.

Arranging entertainment

From ceilidhs to discos

The entertainment at a wedding is a vital part of the celebrations and often takes up a large part of the evening. There are numerous options depending on the bride and groom's taste, the style of wedding, the facilities available and the time of day. For a daytime reception, a harpist and flute duo, a string quartet or a small jazz band is a pleasing option. Their repertoire should be light enough to appeal to a varied age group and never so loud that it overwhelms the conversation.

For the evening entertainment anything goes, from karaoke to a live orchestra, from a jazz band to a raging disco. It is usual for the bride and groom to select the evening entertainment, and although they are likely to value your input, remember that their taste is unlikely to be the same as yours. Alternatively, entertainment agents can organize everything. Reputable agents should be registered with either The Agents Association (Great Britain) or the National Entertainment Agents Council.

Entertainment checklist

For a successful evening make sure that the bride and groom have considered the following:

- What type of entertainment would they like? DJ? Dance band? Cover band?
- How will the band charge? Do they offer any special packages or discounts? Is there a minimum time requirement? Will they play overtime and at what cost? Are travel costs included?
- Who is responsible for feeding the entertainers?
- Does the band have a demo tape or is there a venue where they can be heard performing live?
- In the case of a band, how long have these particular musicians been together and performing at weddings?
- What time will they arrive? How long will it take for them to set up?
- How often do they take breaks and for how long?
- Can taped music be played during breaks?
- What will the musicians be wearing?
- Does the venue have an entertainment licence?
- Can the volume be easily controlled?
- Does the DJ work from a predetermined playlist or will he or she accommodate requests?
- Does the DJ need any equipment?
- How far in advance are bookings required?
- What is the policy on cancellation/postponement?
- What is the deposit to secure the date? When is it due?
- How soon after the event is the balance due?
- Is VAT included in the final price?
- Confirm dates, times and details with a written contract.
- Get insurance.

Sorting food and drink

The catering and refreshments will depend largely on the venue, budget and type of reception. Some venues have resident caterers, others may be able to recommend caterers or will even insist on using a particular one. For a low-key affair, local restaurants, bakers, off-licences and supermarkets will provide you with an estimate. Seriously consider using a professional caterer if your guest list exceeds 20 so you can enjoy the party and not worry about serving food or clearing up afterwards.

Choosing a caterer

Whether you are organizing the caterer or your daughter and her partner are, allow time to get estimates and to compare catering services, facilities and costs. Remember good caterers get booked up months in advance.

A personal recommendation is always the best guide. If the caterer runs a restaurant or hotel, sample a meal before making a decision. Many hotels will let you sample their suggested wedding menus, either for free or at a reduced price, once a booking is made.

The caterer will need to know the date, time of reception, number of guests, level of hospitality and the limit on charges per head in order to supply ideas, sample menus and quotations. Always ask for confirmation of everything in writing.

Don't forget to finalize the numbers with the caterers just before the wedding, otherwise you'll be charged for wasted meals.

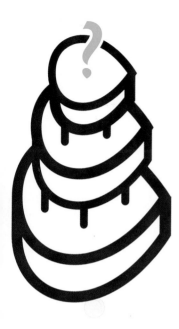

Menu options

Wedding menus vary from a light lunch to an elaborate dinner, with many options in between.

- A finger buffet could include canapés, small sandwiches, individual pastries and dips. The guests do not require cutlery and are free to mingle and eat at the same time.
- A fork buffet can include a wide choice of food with a variety of salads and/or hot dishes. The guests serve themselves and then sit at specific places laid out for them on a seating plan.
- A sit-down meal is the traditional reception fare, but it is also the most expensive option. Usually there will be a minimum of three courses – starter, main course and dessert – plus coffee and cake.

The wedding cake

The traditional wedding cake is a rich fruit cake with thick icing. It's usually square or round and comes in two or three tiers. The wedding cake needs to be ordered well in advance as a multi-tiered cake can take months to create.

It is best for the cake to be delivered to the reception venue unassembled and then the tiers put together in situ. Make sure the venue has somewhere safe to store the cake and that they can assemble it.

If your daughter doesn't want to have a traditional wedding cake then the caterer should be able to suggest a range of alternatives.

Who will make the wedding cake?
The different options are:
- Have a standard cake specially decorated.
- Have the cake made by a specialist.
- Have the cake made by a relative or friend and then iced professionally.
- Have the cake made and iced by a relative or friend.
- Order the cake from a local bakery.

Drinks

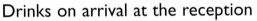

Choosing the drinks to have at your daughter's wedding is an area where your expertise and help will undoubtedly be extremely welcome.

The quantity and type of drinks provided will be determined by the style of the meal, the budget and the number of guests. As well as alcoholic drinks, make sure there are also plenty of non-alcoholic drinks, for children, drivers, older guests, those suffering from the heat and perhaps those suffering from too much champagne!

Drinks on arrival at the reception

It is normal to provide a drink for guests as they arrive at the reception. It may be an aperitif, like a medium or dry sherry, a glass of champagne or sparkling wine, or maybe buck's fizz or Pimm's. There should also be some soft drinks on offer, such as orange juice, especially if there are children at the wedding. For a winter wedding, mulled wine is a welcome option.

Drinks with the meal

At the meal itself, either champagne or sparkling wine can be served, but it is quite normal to have white or red wine, and often a bottle of each is placed on every table. Soft drinks should also be provided, such as orange juice or a more exotic non-alcoholic cocktail. It is also usual for bottles of still and sparkling water to be provided. At an afternoon reception, it would be a good idea to serve tea or coffee at some point.

Drinks for the toasts

It is traditional for a glass of champagne to be served to each guest prior to the speeches, so that they can toast the bride and groom. Alternatively, serve sparkling wine instead of champagne.

Drinks in the evening

If the celebrations go on into the evening, it's quite acceptable to have a pay bar and for the bridal party to put some money behind it. Once that has been spent, guests pay for their own drinks.

Corkage

The caterer or venue may provide the drinks, service and the necessary equipment, but do watch the price. Some venues allow the wedding organizer to provide the drink, but they tend to charge corkage, so there may not be much difference in cost overall.

 If drinks are bought from a supplier, such as an off-licence, make sure it is on a sale-or-return basis. Usually suppliers can advise on the best choice of wines and provide glasses, ice buckets and ice.

Duties on
the big day

Giving your daughter away

This is the moment of truth – although this is a big day for your daughter, it is a big day for you, too. Her marriage marks the beginning of a new and exciting life for her. For you it signals the end of your paternal duties towards your precious little girl – today is the day you give her away. Of course, your daughter may have left home a long time ago, but you are still bound to feel some sort of responsibility towards her. This will not change just because she is getting married, but you must expect the dynamics of your relationship to shift now that she is moving on and has someone else to turn to for support.

The wedding rehearsal

The week or even the day before a church wedding, you will probably be expected to go to the wedding rehearsal which will be attended by the bridal party and possibly the groom's parents.

At the rehearsal, the minister will run through the service, everyone will be shown where to stand before and during the service and the rough timings will be finalized.

As well as being a practice run for the service, the rehearsal also serves as a meeting time for any members of the wedding party who have yet to meet. The bride and groom often take the opportunity to take the wedding party out for dinner as a token of their appreciation. In the US, these 'rehearsal dinners' are the norm.

Share a special moment together

A day or two before the wedding try to spend time alone with your daughter. Talk about the wedding and how exciting it all is. She is probably feeling nervous and it will help to go over the timetable for the day and to check that everything is in place. Tell your daughter what it means to you to be giving her away. Tell her that you and her mother are proud of her and that you both love her. Reiterate the fact that she has made a good choice (you never know, she may be feeling doubtful) and that she is definitely doing the right thing.

If it helps either or both of you, talk about your own wedding day – how you felt when you saw her mother for the first time and what it meant finally to be married. This is all about you and her, and making the day special in more ways than one. It is a time to be open and you may find yourself telling your daughter things that you never dreamt you would say as you reflect on her future.

Fighting back the tears

If there is a wedding rehearsal, use it (quite literally) as a dry run. You may have been so bound up in planning and making arrangements that you have not given any time to thinking just how you might feel when it actually comes to giving your daughter away. A father choked with pride is one thing, a blubbing dad is something else.

The morning of the wedding

Morning has broken

This is going to be one of the most hectic days of your life, so make sure you have organized and double-checked everything the night before. Go over the final version of your speech, and give a spare copy to your wife or another relative in case of disaster.

Things to do

- Double-check all of your transport arrangements and confirm there are no hold-ups. Reassure your daughter you've done this, then see to your own nerves with a (small) glass of champagne.
- If the buttonholes have been delivered to your house, which is the norm, make sure those for the groom, best man and ushers are either collected by the best man, or taken to the groom's house in good time.
- Make sure your daughter's honeymoon suitcase is packed and in the right car, or that the best man takes it when he collects the buttonholes.
- Pander to the women – your daughter, your wife and any bridesmaids. They will be anxious about getting ready and looking their best. Make sure they have everything they need and tell them they all look beautiful.
- When helping your daughter into the bridal car, make sure that her fabulous dress is not crushed.

Getting to the ceremony

Your most important task is to support your daughter, calm her nerves and, above all, get her to the church or register office on time.

You will also need to make sure the cars arrive as arranged to take the bridesmaids, your wife and other members of the family to the ceremony.

Your words of wisdom

The car journey to the ceremony will probably be the only time you have alone with your daughter today, so if you want to say anything to her, now's the time. Most brides are very nervous at this point, so a few words of support will be appreciated. Make sure you've got a few tissues in case either of you is tearful.

Before setting off
Most importantly, arrange for the best man to call you to confirm the groom is on his way to the ceremony venue if he is not there already. Make sure your party leaves for the ceremony venue in the right order and on time. Find somewhere in your wedding suit to pack a hanky or two (for you, your wife, your daughter) and make sure you have your buttonhole.

The wedding ceremony

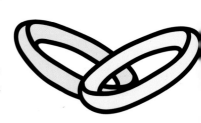

The order of events is the same whether your daughter is having a church ceremony or a civil one. However, it tends to be more formal in a church.

A church wedding

If the ceremony is taking place in a church, then you will enter the church with your daughter and accompany her down the aisle, your arms linked, to the front of the congregation where her fiancé is already waiting. You then join your wife in the front row of the pews on the left-hand side.

Once you have walked your daughter up the aisle a hymn is usually sung. The vicar then states the reason for the gathering and asks if anyone knows of any reason why the marriage should not take place. Having received the couple's agreement to be married, the vicar asks who is giving the bride away. The bride hands her bouquet to her chief bridesmaid, you stand up next to your daughter and then place your daughter's right hand in that of the vicar, who gives it to the groom.

In most church weddings, once the couple are officially husband and wife, you escort the groom's mother to the vestry for the signing of the register. At the end of the ceremony, you follow your wife and the groom's father down the aisle, escorting the groom's mother on your right-hand side.

A civil wedding

If the marriage is taking place at a register office or other licensed wedding venue, it is up to your daughter to decide whether she wants to enter accompanied by you or perhaps her chief attendant, because there is no established etiquette involved. As her father, however, you are the usual choice.

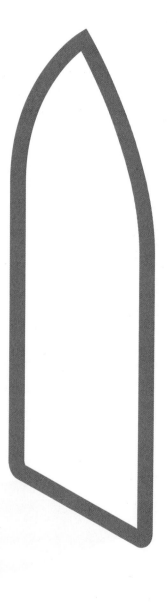

Reception duties

Whether your daughter has a formal wedding and reception or a more informal gathering, most receptions tend to follow a certain pattern.

The receiving line

A traditional formal receiving line is where the bride and groom line up with both sets of parents and greet each guest as they enter the room. It is advisable to go through the guest list together before the day, so that you are acquainted with all the guests' names.

The receiving line can be as the guests leave the wedding ceremony or as they arrive at the reception, which is the most popular choice. If there is a master of ceremonies, they can announce each guest as they enter the room.

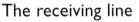

Know your place
When you get to the reception venue, the duties of father of the bride are as follows:
- Deliver any messages to the best man for his speech.
- Head the receiving line, if required, to greet and welcome guests as they move into the reception room.
- Deliver your speech as father of the bride, and toast the bride and groom.

What are the options?

- The conventional receiving line, based on the notion that the bride's parents are paying for the entire wedding, is to have you and your wife first, then the groom's parents and then the bride and groom. The best man and chief bridesmaid are sometimes included at the end of the line.
- For a smaller line, just the bride and groom greet the guests. In this case, your role is to mingle, socialize and introduce guests to each other.
- Alternatively, your daughter may not want to have a receiving line at all. This is her choice, but you might want to suggest to her that it does give her the chance to talk to every guest individually at least once on the day and thank them for coming.

At the reception

If your daughter's wedding is following a traditional pattern, there are some key elements that need to be included in the reception.

As well as the receiving line and the top table, wedding receptions have traditions for opening the dancing, cutting the cake, giving gifts, going home and disposing of the bouquet. Then, of course, there are the speeches.

Speeches and toasts

Most receptions include speeches and toasts. These should always be properly planned, rehearsed and timed. Usually they come at the end of the meal, although there is an increasing trend to have them before the meal begins. Usually, you will speak first and then toast the bride and groom. Next comes the groom – and perhaps the bride. They thank their guests for coming and, traditionally, the groom proposes a toast to the bridesmaids. Then, finally, comes the best man, who officially 'replies' on behalf of the bridesmaids.

Favours

It's usual nowadays to provide each guest with a tiny gift, or favour, to remind them of the wedding day. These range from traditional Italian sugared almonds, more modern confectionery options, such as chocolates or jelly beans, to perfumed candles and even extravagant silver trinkets.

Cutting the cake

The bride and groom cut the cake together as a symbol of their shared future. After the cake-cutting ceremony (usually at the very end of the meal and after the speeches), the caterers remove the cake, which is sliced up and handed round to the guests.

First dance

Traditionally, the bride and groom have the 'first dance' together. This would have been a waltz in the past, but nowadays it's whatever the couple choose. The groom then dances with his new mother-in-law and his mother, while the bride dances with her new father-in-law and you. The best man joins in by dancing with the chief bridesmaid, while the ushers dance with the other bridesmaids.

Timely departure

Guests are supposed to remain at the reception until the newlyweds leave, so if there is to be no formal 'going away', make sure the guests know (especially the older ones) so they don't feel they need to stay all night. As host of the party by tradition you should be the last to leave.

The top table

Traditionally, at the top table at a wedding everyone is seated down one side of a long rectangular table, facing the rest of the room. The usual arrangement is, from the left: chief bridesmaid, groom's father, bride's mother, groom, bride, bride's father, groom's mother, best man. An alternative is for you to sit next to your wife and the groom's parents to sit together.

If there are large numbers of extended family, for example if you and your ex-wife (the bride's mother) have both remarried, then you may need to be a bit more creative with the 'top table' arrangement. It is becoming less and less common to have a formal seating arrangement on the top table, and other options include having a round (non-hierarchical) table or several tables rather than just one.

Remember that the top table is always the focus of attention, and any resentment or bitterness lurking between people, for example current partners and exes, is going to be very obvious. If you have issues with any other members of the top table try to resolve them before your daughter's big day. If this is not possible at least make sure that you are civil to each other.

While your daughter will have done her best to avoid seating sworn enemies next to each other, sometimes it's unavoidable. If this happens, make sure you or your daughter warn each person in advance and trust that their love for the bride and groom will take precedence over their mutual animosity.

Stay focused
While it is easy to get completely absorbed in making your speech and forget about your other duties as father of the bride, it's not in the interests of either your speech or your relationship with the bride to do so. Your role is a multiple one. Hosting the wedding reception, receiving guests, introducing guests to one another and generally making sure everything runs smoothly are all part of your job. If you concentrate on doing these things, you'll not only be fulfilling your role properly, but you'll also be distracting yourself from any pre-speech nerves.

Party time!

Once your big speech is out of the way you can relax a little. Your responsibilities are not over yet, however. You need to keep a general eye on the proceedings. Make sure that everyone is happy and try to talk to as many guests at the reception as you can. If wedding cameras have been put out on the guests' tables, for example, ensure they are used throughout the reception. It is also traditional for you to dance with the bride after the bride and groom have had their 'first dance'.

Finally, it is your job to bring the celebrations to a close, making sure everyone has transport home or can find their room if they are staying overnight at the reception venue. Check the final bill and ensure any outstanding payments are settled at the end of the night. When you leave the venue, take a last look round for any stray presents or lost property.

Checklist of duties on the day

If you have been organized in the months and weeks before the wedding day, everything should fall neatly into place and there shouldn't be any nasty surprises or last-minute emergencies. However, there is still a lot to remember and as father of the bride you are likely to be consumed by nerves on the big day. Here is a checklist to keep you on top of it all:

- Keep a record of all the absent guests and hand this to the best man. It is traditional for him to mention them at the reception.
- Make sure you have your speech notes with you and that you are well rehearsed.
- Make sure you have cash to pay relevant suppliers on the day and that you know exactly how much each is owed.
- Call the car company first thing to make sure the booking is all in order.
- Help the best man with photographs, by making sure your family members are all present and correct on leaving the ceremony venue.
- Get to the reception venue in good time, so that the reception line is ready and waiting by the time the other guests arrive.
- Make sure you have made suitable arrangements for getting home at the end of the day.

Making a
speech

The father of the bride's speech

Your daughter has chosen to marry, and it is your duty to send her into married life by celebrating her pre-wedding years in a sentimental – and possibly amusing – way. You've waited all your life for this moment, so take the time to enjoy it. This is your chance to tell her how much you care for her and let everyone else know how wonderful she is. Make the most of this opportunity.

When you speak

Traditionally, the father of the bride is the first speaker (apart from a brief introduction from the best man), so your speech is a sort of scene-setter. The idea behind this is linked to the fact that the father of the bride was always supposed to foot the bill for the wedding – so if you're paying, you should at least be allowed to get your oar in first.

What to say

- Thank anyone involved in planning (and paying for) the wedding.
- Speak proudly about your daughter and welcome the groom into your family.
- Thank everyone for coming.
- Propose a toast to the bride and groom.

Alternative speeches

- Make a joint speech with your wife.
- Share the stage with a stepfather or godfather.
- Simply thank everyone for coming and propose a toast.
- Show a short film or candid camera shots of your daughter as a child.

Who speaks and when

Traditionally, the toastmaster or master of ceremonies will introduce the speeches at the end of the meal. The formal order of speakers is:

- father of the bride (or a close family friend)
- groom
- best man.

The bride, chief bridesmaid or other guests may want to speak, too. If so, they will usually speak before the best man.

Traditionally, the speeches take place after the meal, but some couples decide to have them beforehand to allow the speakers to enjoy their meal free of nerves.

Cardinal rules

Even if you are unaccustomed to public speaking, as father of the bride you can't get out of making this speech. Stick to the cardinal rules and make your piece a sure-fire success.

Pick the right tone

Tone can be tricky. In making your speech, you have to fulfil certain obligations.

- You need to convey affection and sincerity but avoid coming across as too serious, dull or even pompous.
- Aim to entertain. A speech without humour is a boring thing indeed, but a speech that sounds like a second-rate stand-up comedian on an off-night can be impersonal and lacking in warmth. Be funny, but never risk giving offence.
- The ideal tone is one of gentle humour, intimacy and affection. Try to aim for something that makes everyone feel included.

Keep it short

However fabulous your speech, the golden rule is always to leave your audience wanting more. Wedding guests enjoy speeches, but don't overestimate their boredom threshold. Your performance should, as Oscar Wilde once said, 'be exquisite, and leave one unsatisfied'.

- Stick to quick-fire quips rather than shaggy-dog stories; anecdotes rather than sagas; pithy comments rather than rambling digressions.
- To help you get it right, time yourself when you practise.

Don't wing it

Take time to prepare and write your speech. Keep it in the back of your mind for a few weeks before the wedding and jot down ideas as they occur to you.

- Ask others for anecdotes and use books and quotations, as well as your imagination, to help you create your masterpiece.
- Hone your performance by rehearsing, preferably with people you can rely on for honest, constructive feedback.

Don't mention the war...

Aim to make your speech appeal to everyone and, most importantly, avoid anything that may cause offence.

- You have to include all the guests. If an anecdote can't easily be explained, leave it out.
- Swearing is a definite no-go area. The last thing you need is granny fainting at a four-letter word.
- Finally, whatever feelings you may have about the couple's compatibility or doubts about your new son-in-law, this is definitely not the time to let your hostility show.

Don't ramble or mumble

Keep to your planned speech and deliver it clearly. Avoid swallowing your words, speaking too fast and losing your place (in which case you might as well admit it and get a laugh).

- Create a definite structure with a beginning, middle and end.
- Remember that long drawn-out jokes may fall flat.
- As soon as you start your speech, check that everyone in the room can hear you, then speak slowly and clearly.
- Signal jokes by pausing to allow everyone to laugh.

Good preparation

Preparation is at the heart of a good speech. Unfortunately, scribbling down a few words the night before the big day is not going to work. Start formulating ideas soon after the engagement is announced, but keep them on the back burner and really start working on your speech a few weeks before the wedding.

It's an unfailing rule: the more prepared you are, the more confident you will be about giving your speech, and the more your audience will enjoy it. And the more relaxed you are, the more you'll enjoy the experience, too.

Break down each element

Don't think about your speech as one big lump. Break it down into headings and decide what you're going to say under each one. For instance, recall memories of your daughter as a child, her personality traits and successes, your relationship with her, and how she and her new husband are great together. Then look at all the elements and work out the best order in which to fit them together.

Speech-making aids

As you prepare, make sure you have:

- A notebook so you can jot down ideas as they occur to you.
- A tape recorder so that you can practise your delivery and time your speech.
- Asked friends and family to listen to your speech and give you ideas.
- Decided what props (if any) you are using and how to use them.
- A copy of the latest draft of your speech to carry round with you, so that you can make notes and work on it whenever you want.

What kind of speech?
Decide what kind of speech you want to make before you start putting it together. You could:
- Adopt a well-known format to comic effect.
- Use props.
- Use a home video or slides of your daughter when she was younger.

The right material

Wedding speakers have it tough. Who else has to make a speech that will appeal to an audience with an age range of two to 82? Speeches have to make people laugh without offending anyone's sensibilities, talk about families and relationships without treading on anyone's toes and hold people's attention.

Tips for success

It sounds like a tall order, but most of the pitfalls of speech-making can be avoided if you know what to talk about and recognize that there are limits around certain subjects. It's all a matter of choosing and using your material with care.

Don't be critical

Weddings aren't the place for criticism. Don't make jokes at other people's expense, especially the bride's, even if you know she would find it funny if said to her in private. This is the happy couple's perfect day, and you need to reinforce that. Make sure that you only compliment your daughter, and don't make any jokey remarks about her diet either.

Be kind

Remember, if you're trying to make your speech humorous, then you must also keep it sincere. Talk about how highly you think of your daughter and how her relationship with the groom has enriched both of them. Give the couple all your very best wishes for the future.

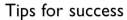

Include everyone

To make sure no one feels left out, imagine all the different types of people who might be listening to your speech and try to include something for everyone. Avoid in-jokes and make sure you explain references to people and places some listeners may not be familiar with.

Tailored to fit

The material that you decide is suitable for your speech will depend on your audience. It's up to you to find out who you'll be talking to, and to ensure what you want to say won't cause offence. If you can rehearse your speech in front of your mum without her feeling uncomfortable or you feeling embarrassed, you're probably on to a winner.

Speech checklist

For a great father of the bride speech, check you have covered the following:

- Is your speech positive and complimentary?
- Have you tested it on other people and asked for their honest feedback?
- Have you timed it to ensure it's not too long?
- Have you been careful not to offend anyone? Or leave anyone out?
- If there is a microphone, do you know how to use it?
- Have you written notes, in case you dry up?
- Have you made a note of everyone you need to thank?

Good delivery

It ain't what you do...

As anyone who's made a successful speech will tell you, it's
not what you say, it's the way you say it. So here's how to
make sure that the way you deliver and present your
speech does justice to your carefully written masterpiece.

Practice makes perfect

Reading your speech out again and again before the big day
is essential if you want to perfect your delivery, ensure
your material is suitable and find out if your jokes are
funny. Your speech should appeal to everyone at the
wedding, so try to rehearse in front of a variety of people.
Test it out on people who will give honest, constructive
feedback. They will also be able to tell you when you're
mumbling, or rambling, or just going on for too long.

You should also record your rehearsals on tape. That
way, you will be able to review yourself and see where
there's room for improvement and how you are for time.

The run-up

The celebrations and reception have begun. Good food and
wine is flowing but all you can think about is how nervous
you are about your imminent speech. How you fill your
time will affect your delivery.

Don't overindulge

Although it's very tempting to down a few too many glasses while you're waiting to speak – don't. Being tipsy could affect your delivery by making you slur your words and cause you to be unsteady on your feet.

Have a banana

Many professional performers swear by the trick of eating a banana about 20 minutes before they start speaking. Doing this, they say, will give you a quick energy boost and help steady your nerves.

Timing

Timing is crucial when it comes to speeches. However brilliant yours is, and however good a speaker you are, five minutes is more than enough. People enjoy listening to speeches, but they also want to get on with talking and dancing, so keep it short. Make sure your speech has a firm beginning, middle and end. Steer clear of rambling stories in favour of short, pithy jokes and asides. When it comes to speeches, less is definitely more.

Useful prompts

Memory joggers

Reading an entire speech from a sheet of paper can make it sound a bit lifeless and can stop you from making eye contact with the audience. One of the ways to get around this is to memorize your speech and use prompts to remind you of what you want to say.

To cut down on the amount of text you use, first write the whole speech out, then make very brief notes that remind you of each part of it. Gradually cut back on your text, so the notes say only as much as you need to jog your memory.

On cue

Make a set of cue cards. These are small index cards with key phrases that remind you of different parts of your speech, stacked in the order that you say them. Inserting blank cards for pauses can help you pace your speech. Even if you feel you need to put your whole speech on cards, they are still preferable to a piece of paper, because you will need to pause and look up as you turn them.

What the experts say

'The more you practise delivering your speech, the less nervous you will be. Practise the pauses, the intonations, the anecdotes. By showing you've put even a little thought and effort into what you're saying, all manner of sins will be forgiven. Recite your speech in the shower. On the bus. On the loo. On the night, your nerves will thank you, because instead of fretting about the audience or your flies, you'll simply focus on what you're going to say.'

Rob Pointer, stand-up comic and serial best man

'Don't speak when you're looking down at your notes. Look down for a moment, look up, smile at everyone, speak – then repeat. You don't need to talk constantly; it gives guests a break, and if you're not afraid of silence, you'll look confident, so everyone can relax. Remember that in between speaking, silence feels approximately ten times longer than it is, so take it nice and slow.'

Jill Edwards, comedy coach and scriptwriter

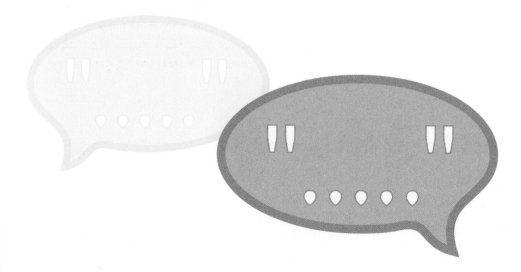

Ten steps to success

Before you start panicking, remember that weddings are happy occasions and all the guests want to see everything go well, including your speech. Be assured, the audience is on your side, they're all rooting for you, so make the most of it and use their goodwill to boost your confidence.

1 Make eye contact

Make eye contact when you're making your speech – just not with everyone at once. Try to speak as if you were talking to one person and focus on them. You can look around the room if you want to, but focus on one person at a time. The trick is to imagine that you're simply chatting to someone.

2 Don't look down

Even if you decide to learn your speech off by heart, you will need to have some notes to refer to in case your mind goes blank in the heat of the moment. However, don't deliver your speech while hiding behind a quivering piece of paper or constantly staring downwards. Look down for a moment, look up and speak. Get into a rhythm of doing this throughout your speech.

3 Breathe properly

When people get nervous, they tend to swallow their words; this can render a beautifully written speech nearly inaudible. You don't want to deliver your speech only to find that no one could actually hear what you were saying. An effective way to combat the mumbling menace is by breathing properly – take deep, rhythmic breaths, as this will pump oxygen into your blood and keep your brain sharp and alert. Check that you're audible by arranging beforehand for someone at the back of the room to signal when your voice isn't carrying.

4 Set a good pace

Gabbling is another thing people tend to do when they're nervous. To stop yourself talking too fast, write the word 'pause' at intervals throughout your notes, or if you are using cue cards, insert blank ones that will automatically cause you to slow down. If you do lose your place, it's best just to make a joke of it.

5 Time your jokes

Pause briefly after you make a joke to give people a chance to laugh, but keep jokes and anecdotes short so that if one doesn't work, you can move on quickly to the next. If your joke dies, don't despair. Turn the situation to your advantage by inserting a quip such as 'Only me on that one then', or look round at an imaginary assistant and say: 'Start the car!' Rescue lines like these can earn you a chuckle from a momentarily awkward silence.

6 Remember to smile

Making a speech is supposed to be fun, so make sure you don't look utterly miserable when you're doing it. Smile! Think of something that makes you laugh before you start speaking to get yourself in the right mood. Body language is crucial, too, so adopt a relaxed posture before you begin – no crossed arms or fidgeting.

7 Start strongly

Opening lines are important, because they grab the audience's attention and get you off to a good start. Something like: 'Ladies and gentlemen, they say speeches are meant to be short and sweet, so thank you and good night,' should help you to begin in style.

8 Think positively

Instead of seeing your speech as a formal ordeal, think of it as being a conversation between you and a lot of people you know and really like. Thinking positively about your speech and the reason why you are there will help you to deliver it with confidence and make the task seem less intimidating.

To help calm your nerves, imagine your speech being over and everyone applauding. Imagine how you'll feel when you can sit down, relax and really enjoy the rest of the evening. By visualizing everything going well, you should gain even more confidence.

9 Convey your message

Think about the meaning of your speech while you're making it. Concentrate on the thoughts you want to convey and the message behind your words, rather than just reciting your notes, as this will help you to make your delivery much more expressive and sincere.

10 End with a toast

End your speech with a toast to the bride and groom. This will give it a focus and provide something to work towards. After you make your toast, you can sit down when everyone else sits down, signifying a definite end to your speech.

Stage fright

It's only natural to be nervous. If you find that you're really scared when you begin, don't panic. Make a joke out of it instead. Lines like 'This speech is brought to you in association with Imodium' or 'I was intending to speak but my tongue seems to be welded to the roof of my mouth' should raise a laugh and will help to get the audience on your side.

One completely bald father of the bride started off on a high note by remarking: 'As you can see, I've been so worried about making this speech, I've been tearing my hair out.' There's no shame in admitting you're a little scared.

Wedding speech checklist

Follow the steps in this checklist to ensure that your speech goes superbly on the big day.

Once you've agreed to speak
- Start thinking about what you want to say.
- Think about the audience. Your speech will have to appeal to a wide range of people.
- Make sure nothing in your speech will cause offence.
- Ask friends and family for funny stories/embarrassing pictures that you can build into your speech.
- Keep your speech in the back of your mind. You never know when you might recall a good story.
- Keep a notebook to hand to jot down ideas.
- Speak to friends who have made wedding speeches before and find out what not to do.
- Decide on the kind of speech you want. Will you need any props or visual aids or any equipment?

The build-up
- Think about the structure. Would the speech be better broken down into manageable chunks/themes?
- Does your speech do what it's supposed to do? Is it affectionate, charming and humorous without being offensive?
- Have you included everything you need to say in your speech?
- Gather any props/presentation aids you'll need and make sure you know how to use them.
- Build in plenty of time to practise your speech.

Only a week to go

- Use a tape recorder or video to record yourself.
- Rope in an audience of friends to practise on.
- Be sure to practise your speech with any props you plan to use – winging it on the day is not a good bet.
- Time your speech. Aim to keep it to around five minutes.
- Write your speech in note form on cue cards, even if you intend to commit it to memory.
- Think positively about your speech and it will feel like less of an ordeal.
- Visualize your speech being over and everyone applauding your performance as this will help to give you confidence and calm your nerves.
- Remember the audience is on your side – you'll be able to use their goodwill to boost your confidence.

The big day

A few last pointers to help your speech go smoothly:
- Try to relax and take it easy.
- Try not to look for Dutch courage in the bottom of your wine glass – you'll do your speech more harm than good!
- Keep busy with your other duties; this will help keep away those pre-speech nerves.
- Have your notes with you, even if you've committed your speech to memory. If your mind goes blank or you feel yourself veering off the point, at least you can refer to them, to get back on track.
- End your speech with the toast – it will be a clear signal that your bit is over.

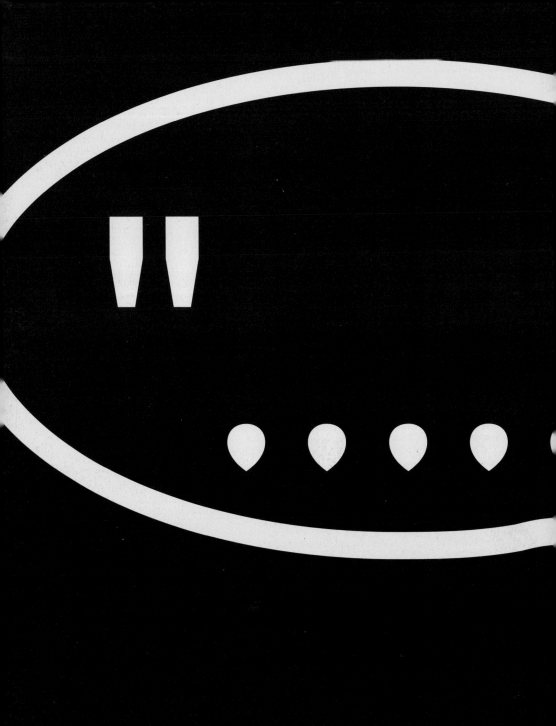

Great

speech
material

The basics

Expectations of your speech

The father of the bride's speech is generally expected to be the least funny and often the most sentimental of the wedding speeches, which should make the job of writing it the easiest. However, this is not always the case. Your speech is often the one that has been anticipated for the longest period of time and is probably, if not the most emotional, then certainly the one filled with the most pride.

The father of the bride usually begins the speeches, thus setting the tone for the rest of the proceedings. The best advice is to stick largely with convention, unless you are feeling particularly brave or imaginative. It's easiest to write a speech using the traditional component parts: welcoming the guests, thanking everyone, talking about the bride, welcoming the groom and, finally, making the toast.

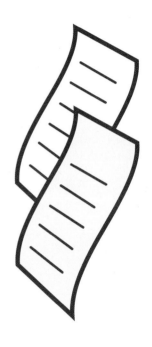

So what do you have to say?
- Thank the guests for coming to the wedding and being involved in such a special day. Remember to mention anyone who has travelled a long distance.
- Thank anyone who has made some kind of financial contribution to the wedding.
- Tell your daughter how proud you are of her.
- Welcome your new son-in-law into your family.
- Reminisce about your daughter's pre-wedding years.
- Wish the newlyweds success and happiness in the future.
- Propose a toast to the bride and groom.

Useful phrases

Here are various suggestions to consider incorporating into your wedding speech.

1 The welcome

- 'Thank you all for coming and sharing this special day with Nicola and John.'
- 'I'd like to take this opportunity to thank you all for being here. I know that some of you have had further to come than others, but you are all welcome guests on this happy day/night.'
- 'Ladies and gentlemen, I'm delighted to see so many of you here today to celebrate the marriage of my daughter Nicola to John.'

2 The thanks

- 'Nicola and John have worked very hard to pay for today and it's been worth it. This is a lovely meal/reception and everything looks perfect. I'm proud of the pair of you.'
- 'Weddings are not cheap occasions, but my little girl/daughter deserves the best and, as you can see, she's got it. This would not have been possible without the generous help of John's parents, George and Amy.'

- 'This wedding has taken a lot of time and patience to organize, and decisions have sometimes been difficult to reach (make a small joke about the struggle it was to decide between a sophisticated colour scheme or an outrageous one of pink with yellow spots), but I'm really delighted that everything's turned out so well. In particular, I'd like to thank the florist/minister/bridesmaids for the amount of trouble they have gone to. Everything/the flowers/the church/the hall/the hotel looks wonderful.'

3 The bride

- 'I have always known that Nicola is a beautiful woman, but I have never seen her look quite so gorgeous or so radiant as she does today. I'm extremely proud of her.'
- 'Nicola has had many roles in life… (for example, daughter, sister, student, lawyer), but never has she looked more lovely than as a bride.'
- 'When Nicola told me that she was going to get married, I was worried that she wouldn't be my little girl any more, but seeing her today as a beautiful bride, I realize that no matter how old she is she will always be my baby and I love her.'
- 'This elegant/beautiful/radiant/lovely bride is a far cry from the Nicola I remember so well, who was always in trouble for being messy/muddy/late/a tomboy/scruffy, but, no matter what she looks like, I love her and am very proud to be her father.'

Standing in for the father of the bride
If you're not the bride's father, there are many ways to convey how proud you are to take on this role.

- 'I am not Nicola's father but I know that he would have been so proud of her today, as I am.'
- 'Nicola has always been a joy in my life and I am honoured that she chose me to give this speech.'
- 'As Nicola's big brother, I am supposed to be nasty to her and pull her hair to remind her that I am older than she is. Trouble is, she looks too gorgeous today. I am very proud to be giving her away on behalf of our family. John, please look after her!'

4 Welcome the groom

- 'There are not many men good enough for Nicola, but John is. When she turned up with a scruffy/spotty/runny-nosed/well-groomed/lanky/large/tall/pony-tailed man, I was suspicious/delighted/dismayed/curious/welcoming, and/but I never hoped/really hoped that they would marry. And/But they have and I am thrilled for them. John is a good/delightful/fun/great/lovely man and they make a wonderful couple.'

- 'John is one of that rare breed of men – he really is as good/sincere/wonderful/perfect/much of a creep as he appears and I am absolutely delighted to welcome him into our/my family.'

- 'Nicola always claimed that she would never get married/find the right man/love anyone/be happy, but she was wrong. In John she has found the perfect partner and I am delighted he has become a part of my/our family.'

- 'What can I say about John? He is a great/perfect/lovely/wonderful/good man and no one else would be as perfect for my daughter/Nicola. I'm delighted that he's decided to become part of the family.'

5 General chat

This is your chance to make a few gentle jokes, but nothing crude or offensive. You might even want to quote something or recite a poem.

- 'Marriage is all about compromise, and to keep things running smoothly it is good to talk. However, as Helen Rowland said, "Before marriage, a man will lie awake thinking about something you said; after marriage, he'll fall asleep before you finish saying it."'

- 'The best guarantee for a peaceful marriage is simple – lie. If she asks you if you've done whatever you've forgotten to do, say that you have and then do it. If he catches you doing something you shouldn't, say you did it as a surprise for him. Men are stupid: they'll believe anything, or at least pretend to, for a peaceful life!'

- 'Nicola always said that she'd never find that special someone, but I'm delighted to see that she has. I just want to read something now because it seems so appropriate and expresses exactly what I mean. It's called "Destiny" and is by Sir Edwin Arnold:

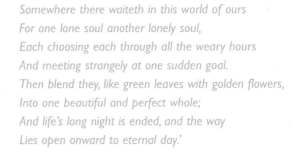

Somewhere there waiteth in this world of ours
For one lone soul another lonely soul,
Each choosing each through all the weary hours
And meeting strangely at one sudden goal.
Then blend they, like green leaves with golden flowers,
Into one beautiful and perfect whole;
And life's long night is ended, and the way
Lies open onward to eternal day.'

- 'You may think that this wedding has cost a lot but, as Goethe said, "The sum which two married people owe to one another defies calculation. It is an infinite debt, which can only be discharged through all eternity." I wonder if their bank manager would believe that?'
- 'As a certain German philosopher once said: "To marry is to halve your rights and double your duties", but if that were all there is to it, then none of us would get married in the first place. I'm delighted that Nicola and John have taken the plunge, otherwise none of us would be here enjoying this fine champagne/wine/beer/tap water.'

6 The toast

By the time you get to the toast, it's almost time for you to sit down – but not quite. Finish with a flourish and then relax – the rest of the reception is yours to enjoy.

- 'Ladies and gentlemen, please be upstanding. I give you... the bride and groom.'
- 'Ladies and gentlemen, please charge your glasses. I give you... the bride and groom.'
- 'Honoured guests, please join me in the traditional toast. I give you... the bride and groom.'
- 'Ladies and gentlemen, please be upstanding and raise your glasses. I give you... the bride and groom.'

About the bride

She's one in a million

'My little girl is one in a million. She's beautiful, like a never-ending summer's day. She's got the patience of a saint. She's intelligent, funny and has an amazing grasp of current affairs and politics. She can cook like **Nigella Lawson**, play golf like **Nick Faldo** and dance like **Darcey Bussell**.'

'Rob, I can say with my hand on my heart that you're one of the luckiest men alive. (*To be said aside to groom.*) And she writes a cracking Father of the Bride speech as well…'

'Anyone who knows my daughter – and I assume that's all of you here, unless you're gate-crashing (in which case, pay attention) – knows that she is quite simply, one in a million. Which by my reckoning means there's only another 50 or so like her in the country. So, any single lads out there, I'd get your skates on, get out there and try to track one down for yourself!'

'I think you'll all agree that Lisa – my little girl – is one in a million. She certainly is to my wife and me, and I know Tim thinks so, too. She's always been a daughter to be proud of – but, more than that, she's a great inspiration to everyone around her. My wife Helen and I are both immensely proud of her.'

Daddy's girl

'Katie was the kind of child any father would be proud of. She excelled in music, was popular at school, was respectful to her seniors and protective of those younger than her. Darling... (*turns to the mother of the bride*) are you sure she's mine?'

'When Emma was born, I shed a tear or two for my beautiful new daughter. On her first day at school, I think I cried more than her. And when she showed me her GCSE results, I was inconsolable with happiness.'

'Sarah was always a tomboy. I think her first words were "Manchester United". As a child, she was never happier than when she was climbing a tree or heading a ball. I can hardly believe that the vision of loveliness before me today is my daughter. You'll never manage a decent goal kick in that frock though, love.'

'The house has seemed very quiet since Karen left home. You can barely hear anything but the sound of my wallet sighing with relief.'

Proud father

'They say that your own wedding is the best day of your life and ours was certainly wonderful. But I think my wife would agree that the wedding day of our lovely daughter has been even better. It's just marvellous to see her so happy. Take my word for it – being the father of the bride is great. I think I'd better stop eating and drinking before I burst with pride.'

'Elizabeth has always had a reputation for being rather choosy. Only the best would do when it came to clothes, hairstyles and cars – and believe me, she's given me a few grey hairs in my time. But I'm certainly glad she was choosy in her choice of groom. Paul is a man to gladden any father-in-law's heart, and I know he'll make my daughter happy.'

'Whatever people might say, it's not all sugar and spice and all things nice with daughters. In fact, Laura has brought home her fair share of slugs and snails, but she's always given us so much joy and never more so than today. She's found the right man and we couldn't be happier for them both.'

She wears the trousers

'It will come as no surprise to you, Adam, that Carina
was nicknamed "Miss Bossy Boots" at school. Looking
back, I suppose she was displaying her leadership
abilities even then. She certainly led my wife and me
up the garden path many a time!'

'Jo was always strong-willed. Even as a child, if there
was something she wanted, she didn't stop until she
got it. So, Nigel, I guess you didn't stand a chance. But
then again, where would Nigel be without someone
there to run his life for him?'

'Tomboy she used to be, lady she is now. But don't be
fooled by that beautiful smile. Sara is a formidable
opponent. Woe betide anyone who disagrees with her.
Ladies and gentlemen, I'm afraid you'll have to forgive
me for the following gap in my speech – Sara edited
the next bit out and I'm under strict instructions not
to mention... er, sorry, that's been crossed out too.'

About the groom

When he was a kid

'I've heard that John was a precocious child. He walked and talked before he was one; he could read and write by the time he was four and could forge his parents' signature by the time he was eight!'

'Malcolm, the groom's father, has been regaling me with stories about Jim's childhood, and I feel it would be rude of me not to share one of them with you today. Apparently Jim was the primary school Romeo. Not that you'd believe it today, but I'm told that he used his "special powers" to get the girls to kiss him. From what Claire's told me about his dubious chat-up routine, it sounds like he abandoned his "special powers" in favour of "Special Brew"…'

'Given that Lucy and George grew up together, I'm in the rare position of having known my new son-in-law since he was a babe in arms. And what a babe he was! I'm not saying he was ugly, but why else would his granny have knitted all those blue full-face balaclavas?'

He's mad about...

'When I found out that Luke had a first-class degree from Oxford, I was naturally quite pleased. When Sophie told me that he had been tipped for the board I was pleasantly surprised. But when she told me he was a Bolton Wanderers season-ticket holder, I went ballistic!'

'Apparently, Steve's a bit of a gadget freak. If it's small, slim and gives you non-stop information 24/7, he's got to have it. And now I come to think of it, I can see exactly what attracted him to Lizzie.'

'Andrew, like me, is mad about motorsport. We've bonded over team victories, fallen out over our Top Ten Drivers of All Time lists and shared tears when Murray Walker retired. So when Andy was setting a wedding date, he checked with me first that the big day didn't clash with a race day. But I'd just like to say to those cynics out there who've noticed that their honeymoon is in Monte Carlo – where I'll be joining them for a day or two – that this is pure coincidence.'

He's not squeaky clean

'When I was first introduced to Jim I thought he was a fine, upstanding man. He treated me with respect, did the whole down-on-one-knee thing, bought me a fine bottle of vintage claret and told me how much he adored my daughter. What a gentleman... or so I thought! It turns out that he'd downloaded a "How to suck up to your future father-in-law" checklist from the Internet. I only know this because I came across it whilst searching for a "How to make your future son-in-law squirm" list.'

'Much to Jeremy's embarrassment, I've been talking to his mother. We've spent ages comparing notes on our respective offspring and now both sets of parents feel much better informed. Apparently squeaky-clean Jeremy wasn't always such a smooth-talking, sharp-suited, go-getter. In fact, I believe his first suit was bought for his first court appearance.'

'When Nick invited Claire's mother and me over to a dinner that he'd cooked, we thought she'd landed herself a New Man. What we didn't know was that he'd defrosted a pie Claire had made previously and just garnished it with a sprig of parsley.'

He's a couch potato

'I'd always imagined my daughter marrying a high-flying, thrusting executive who'd spend his working week flying around the world. But that's not exactly how you'd sum up Brian. Now there are plenty of jobs where you're forced to sit down all day, but most of them involve a desk and an office. However, Brian tells me that I'm still stuck in the twentieth century – that real men now work from home, from their sofa. I'm not sure whether I'm behind the times, or he's a complete layabout. That said, at least he's always there for Sophie when she gets back from work – even if he's watching *Neighbours*!'

'I'm not saying my son-in-law's lazy, but he sent one of his friends to ask me for my daughter's hand in marriage. So I exacted my revenge by sending my response in an enormous box – thereby obliging Matt to get off his behind and go and collect it from the post office depot.'

About their relationship

Great team

'There is great teamwork in everything that they do. Whether it's redecorating the bathroom or choosing a honeymoon, they are able to work together at close quarters for hours on end without a sign of irritation or tension...'

'Helen and I knew right from the outset that these two would make a great team, and we've been proved right. They work hard for each other and don't seem to grumble or moan about anything. And that is the sign of a winning team. This is, of course, a whole new concept to Gerry, him being a Tottenham fan and all...'

'Bobby and Belinda make a perfect team. They always put each other first, and never let other worries get in the way of their relationship. When one of them has a success, the other is there to celebrate. And when one of them is down, the other is there to comfort them. I'm constantly amazed by their closeness and real, heartfelt intimacy.'

How they've changed each other...

'What you are looking at here today is a couple that make a great pair. Like cheese and onion. Or salt and vinegar. And like a bag of crisps left open, since Ben met Angie, he's gone all soft.'

'Since Lynne and Keith have been together you can see the effect they've had on each other. Keith no longer wears the same T-shirt every day, his "Star Trek" collection is in storage and his feet smell less. And as for Lynne, she has... lowered her expectations!'

'Carol and Fred are great together, but it's worth remembering that in marriage one partner often becomes like the other. I'm not sure which would be worse – Carol ending up bald with a beard, or Fred with painted fingernails and earrings.'

About the family

Heartfelt thanks

'When my daughter told us she was getting married, she said: "Don't worry, George and I will organize everything." And we thought, "Yeah, right!" We had visions of sitting down to eat the one thing Anna can actually cook – cheese on toast. But today has made me more proud than ever of my little girl… so thank you, Anna and George, for an elegant, wonderful occasion!'

'My daughter is, as you know, somewhat independently minded. In fact, she and Eddie have insisted on paying for today themselves. Obviously, my wife and I offered, but would they accept our help? No! Eventually, they agreed we could pay for one thing… this ornamental cake knife… (Picks up the item and looks at it.) I must say, you don't get much for five grand these days! Seriously, though, they did do it all themselves – and hasn't it been wonderful?'

'I think there comes a time in any father's life when he has to accept that he doesn't have all the answers. But that's OK. Because his wife does! I think we'd all agree she has done us proud today…'

Coming together

'It's a pleasure to be able to welcome you all here to celebrate the marriage of Jessica and Nick. One of the best things about today is that we've been able to bring all our family and friends together to mark this joyous occasion. We hope that you'll all thoroughly enjoy our special day.'

'Weddings are a marvellous excuse for a big party, and today is no exception. We have a simply enormous crowd here – aunts, uncles, cousins, friends… I think I even recognize a few of you!'

'They say that one of the best things about weddings is the way they bring families together. Well, that's certainly true of this one. People have come here today from far and wide – France, the US, Spain… I believe there may even be some from Manchester.'

'Seeing all the members of my family in one place is quite a novelty. Modern life is so busy that we're all usually rushing off in separate directions. The celebration of Polly and Nathan's marriage gives us a great chance to relax and enjoy each other's company.'

People we miss

Greetings from...

'I have here a message from my brother Ted, who cannot be here today because of poor health. Ted has asked me to pass on his best wishes to the happy couple, and to remind Gavin that everyone here would be delighted to hear his charming Marmite and Swarfega story... Are you all right, Gavin? You look a trifle pale...'

'I'd like to read now a postcard from my son, Colin – Toby's brother – who's currently on active service at an undisclosed location (or so he says). "Sorry I can't be there bruv, but these Hollywood award ceremonies are a real killer. I swear if I have to attend another star-studded, all-night pool party, I'm going to go mad! Anyway, enjoy tonight's barn dance"...'

Sadly, they couldn't be here…

'It's wonderful to see so many people who've travelled so far to come and join us in our celebrations today. Sadly, Bob and Alice were unable to get over from Australia, and they are sorely missed today. But I know that they're thinking about us today, and raising a glass to Kate and Jim even as we speak. Or they will when they wake up, anyway!'

'I speak for everyone when I say how much we miss my mum, who sadly can't be with us today because of ill-health. Mary has always been the life and soul of the party, so she'll be particularly upset to miss out on today's knees-up! But thanks to the wonders of technology, we'll be going round to visit her tomorrow with edited video highlights of today's action…'

'Seeing my daughter look as radiant as she does on her wedding day makes me happier than I ever thought possible. I am so proud of everything that she has become. My only regret is that her mother, Angela, cannot be with us. But this is not a day for regrets – it is a day for happiness and looking ahead.'

Honeymoon advice

Fatherly advice

'Before I left for my own honeymoon, my father gave me two pieces of advice. Number one, don't forget to take protection with you, and number two, make sure your underwear befits the occasion. How right he was: both the umbrella and the thermal vest came in very handy during our week in Bognor.'

'Before you whisk my daughter off to the sun, I'd like to offer you some advice. Don't let her drink too much and do karaoke; remember to tell her she looks brown, even if she's gone a lovely shade of embarrassed lobster; and above all, never, ever laugh at her passport photo.'

'Dave, you're probably expecting a fortnight of relaxation and carefree abandon, but take it from me as one who knows, if your back recovers after hauling Karen's suitcases around the airport, you'll soon put it out again when she asks you to load up the shop's worth of souvenirs she'll want to take home.'

Send us a postcard

'As you get ready for your first holiday as man and wife, I want to wish you a very happy honeymoon. Don't think of us at home, fretting over how we're going to pay for today. And don't forget to send us a postcard. It'll contrast nicely with all the bills on the doormat.'

'Of course you'll be far too busy visiting historical ruins and scuba diving to call home every day, but perhaps you could send your old man a postcard just to let him know you're having a good time.'

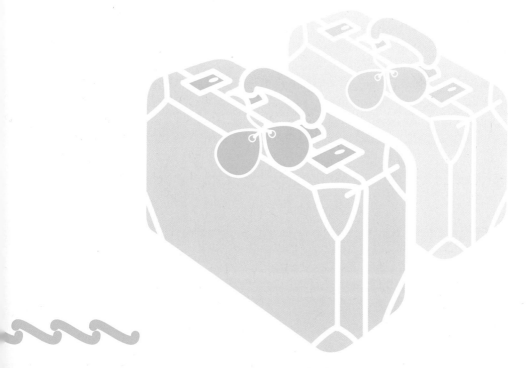

Making a marriage last

Marriage is like…

'Marriage is like an Ordnance Survey map: although it's sometimes difficult to navigate, you'd be lost without it.'

'Marriage to me is like a log fire. When you feel cold, it heats you up, puts warmth in your heart and a glow on your cheeks.'

'On my silver wedding anniversary it occurred to me – a happily married homeowner – that marriage is much like a mortgage. It's expensive and stressful, and initially you may have to deny yourself life's luxuries to make it work. But after 25 years, it all pays off and you've got something you can truly call your own.'

'Marriage is like a pair of your granddad's old slippers, comfortable and familiar.'

'Marriage is like a sketchbook whose pages get filled up over the years. On your wedding day you begin with a blank sheet of paper and a pencil, poised to create true beauty.'

My secret is...

'Anna, your mother and I are so pleased that you and Roger have finally tied the knot, and although you've never taken any advice from me in the past, I'm hoping that today you'll make an exception. I've been married for 30 years, so believe me, I know what I'm talking about. The secret is simple: honesty, trust, love and affection.'

'Nick, I'm sure that throughout your life, wise people have assured you that as long as you communicate honestly with women and let them know what's on your mind, you'll find you have fulfilling and rewarding relationships with them. That's true to a certain extent, but I'd like to update the theory to be more specific to my daughter. By all means communicate with Anna. But remember, just like her mother, she's always right.'

In days gone by...

'In the Stone Age, Mrs Cavewoman stuck by the side of Mr Caveman for a number of reasons. These ranged from the display of virility Mr Caveman showed when he hunted and killed wild boar for dinner, to the endearing nurturing instinct Mrs Cavewoman showed when bringing cave babies into the world. But I think the real reason that marriages lasted in caveman times was because at that point no one had invented the remote control.'

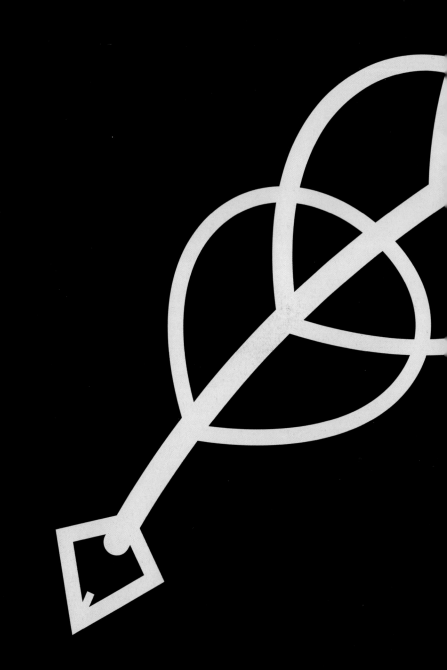

Sample
speeches

Sample speech 1
Reality show relationship

'Ladies and gentlemen, I'm delighted to see so many of you here today to witness the marriage of my wonderful daughter Sarah to my fine new son-in-law John. I'd also like to thank the friends and families on both sides for all their work in the preparation and planning of this glorious event. You are all extremely welcome on this day of all days, a day that warms both my heart and my wife Jill's.

Now, as all her friends will know, Sarah's favourite television programme is the reality show *Big Brother*. And, as much as it shames me to admit it, I too have learnt things from this crazy show. Today, as my darling girl leaves the nest, I can draw similarities between the Big Brother house and our own home, as I reflect on the lessons they've taught me over both 12 weeks and 25 years respectively. There are lessons here for all who make the bold commitment to live and share the daily toils of a life together and a journey in partnership.

There have been many times in the last 25 years, living in a confined space, when my daughter and I have wanted to put each other "up for eviction". Many's the time when, having brought a teenage party to a sensible conclusion at 11pm, I've heard her and her friends chant: "Get dad out, get dad out!"

Many's the time that the need for support of other "housemates" in a domestic spat has led to "tactical voting". And yes, many's the time that both of us have wanted to pack our suitcases and walk. Yet our shared love

has always won through and the peace, thankfully, has always been restored.

Let me also reflect on the perilous pitfalls of "the shopping budget" and "the weekly task". Aged 12, Sarah became a rebel when I refused to order a Chinese takeaway every night or buy her gallons of freshly squeezed orange juice. The words "too expensive" and "be economical" fell on deaf ears.

But now, at 25, it is *she* who cooks us her own sweet and sour pork and provides us with fresh orange juice, which *she* has squeezed herself!

Once upon a time, a "weekly task", be it tidying her room or mowing the lawn, would be another recipe for mutiny and revolution. But now it is *she* who offers me a helping hand with my runner beans at the allotment or

happily picks up my often-forgotten copy of *Hi-Fi News* from the newsagent. What a journey! What a housemate!

Of course, every series of *Big Brother* has a winner, and they have often mirrored Sarah's own journey from shy child to the wonderful, caring and considerate woman she is today. All share something with Sarah, whether it's the cheeky and playful charisma of Brian, the courage and determination of Nadia or the compassion and sheer warmth of her favourite housemate of all, Pete.

Sarah, we cheered them all as they exited the Big Brother house in triumph and today I cheer you, my sweetheart, as you leave our house and enter yours and John's, with our encouragement, support and undying love forever in your heart.

Ladies and gentlemen, I give you... the bride and groom!'

Sample speech 2
Love blossoms

'First of all, Mary (*bride's mother*) and I would like to welcome you all here to celebrate Emma and Richard's marriage. It really is marvellous to see so many old friends here today.

We are sure you will agree with us that Emma looks an absolute picture. But those of you who know her well might be surprised to see that she is wearing a dress rather than dungarees, and is carrying a beautiful bouquet of flowers rather than a spade and trowel. For the love of Emma's life, at least until she met Richard, was gardening.

Indeed, one of my earliest memories of her – she would have been about three – is standing in our garden watching her tearing the heads off the roses. I thought it was just another case of toddler vandalism. But no – when I started to tell her off, she came up to me and said, "Daddy, rose gone", meaning, I think, that the roses had lost their bloom and we had to take the heads off.

It is astonishing and wonderful to me to think that that little gardener, all serious and intent, has become the lovely girl that we see before us today.

As you know, Emma has always been a very enthusiastic and talented gardener, and plants have always been a part of her life. When we first moved to our current house, I remember her running out into the garden and reorganizing everything. Roses should be planted *here*; just *here* would be an excellent place for a herb garden; Daddy would like a little patio for his evening gin and tonic just *here*.

And she was right on all three counts, especially the last one. A lesson for Richard there, perhaps.

Of course, it was a great loss to us when Emma moved out and went to live in London. There was nobody to do the weeding, apart from anything else. I swear the plants were as dismayed as we were. It's one thing having a full-time (if unpaid) gardener living on the premises – it's quite another just seeing her occasionally at the weekend. You might say we were all pining.

But of course, like the plants she cared for, Emma blossomed. The gauche little girl who went away to college disappeared, to be replaced by the confident and beautiful woman you see here today.

And Emma, of course, found her great love in London – not Richard (yet), but her allotment. And those of us who have seen her working away late in the evening, or have been lucky enough to eat the produce from her work, will know how much she puts into it.

When Emma brought Richard to meet us for the first time, we noticed that she treated him rather as she would one of her favourite blooms, with a mixture of respect and love and a certain amount of "You'll do as I say!" And now that their love has flowered, we are all here today to celebrate their marriage.

So it is my happy duty, as father of the bride, to propose…'

Sample speech 3
The fashion queen

'Ladies and gentlemen, it is with great pleasure and a very happy heart that I welcome you all to today's joyous event, the marriage of my beloved daughter Martha to our fine new son-in-law Jack. My wife Susan and I particularly want to thank all the family and friends on both sides, who've given so generously of their time and energy in making today so special. You are all very welcome indeed.

First, I want to take a moment to express my feelings on the significance of today's event and shine a light on the loving spirit that is "my Martha".

Now, as all who know and love Martha will be only too aware, my daughter's driving passion in life is fashion. Clothes, designers, labels, accessories… you name it, she's bought it, worn it, modified it and ultimately passed it on to Oxfam. Indeed, I'm probably the only old "has-been" that she hasn't donated to charity – though at times I'm sure it's come close.

Martha's love of the new and the trendy has imbued her life with an excitement and a sense of glamour that's been infectious to all around her. When has Martha not got a cheery smile on her face? When is she not infused with an optimism that spreads to all who encounter her?

Even as a child, my darling daughter was every bit the fashion queen. Bath time wasn't so much an exercise in cleanliness, more an opportunity to parade up and down in a variety of multicoloured towels and dressing gowns. I can't tell you the number of times her schoolteachers wrote to us complaining about her constant refusal to adhere to strict dress codes; or my countless and futile attempts to persuade her that ra-ra skirts and platform heels weren't the order of the day at St Wilfrid's Comprehensive!

Martha's teens were a veritable showcase of all that was fashionable in Paris, New York and Milan. Trouble was, her avant-garde taste didn't really cut it in downtown Bexhill-on-Sea.

I must confess that I wasn't much support either. I was utterly useless when it came to Martha's eternal quest to emulate the Linda Evangelistas and Christy Turlingtons of this world. "Oh *Dad!*" was a familiar response to my hackneyed suggestions as to which top went with which skirt. But she got her own back when at 18 she took me clothes shopping.

It's probably fair to say, when it comes to fashion, that I'm a belt-and-braces sort of chap. So to be led by the hand into a branch of Benetton and forced to buy what, in her opinion, every trendy "dad about town" should be wearing was a nightmare of cosmic proportions. I came out of the shop looking like a cross between Peter Stringfellow and Keith Chegwin. It took a week before my wife stopped laughing.

Still, Martha's intentions, as always, were heartfelt. As fabulous as Martha looks on the outside, her caring and encouraging heart within is even more radiant.

Martha, thank you my sweetheart. You've taught us so much. And although I still don't know my Lagerfeld from my Prada or my Mango from my Versace, I know I love you with all my heart and wish you and Jack a life of joy, fulfilment and peace.

Ladies and gentlemen, I give you... the bride and groom!'

Sample speech 4

A physical union

'First of all, I'd like, on behalf of Eleanor (*bride's mother*) and myself, to welcome you all here today. It is wonderful to see so many familiar faces, and we hope that at the end of the meal we'll be able to have a word with you all. It really is a great sight to see you all here.

We'd also like to take this opportunity to welcome Mark into the family. Actually, he's been part of the family for a while now. But it gives us great pleasure to make it official!

We'd also like to say how proud we are of Becky (*the bride*) and how wonderful she is looking today. She tells me it's the happiest day of her life, and it's one of the very happiest days of our lives, too.

I am very proud of my daughter's achievements. A few weeks ago, I was in Oxford attending a conference where Becky was due to speak. There was a cocktail party on the first evening, and I happened to overhear two scientists talking about Becky. One of them said "Oh, that's Rebecca Shaw, she's the main speaker tomorrow."

And the other said, "Yes, mind like a steel trap."

I imagine for a physicist, that's a compliment, but the images that floated into my mind at that second were rather different.

I suppose I was thinking about today and the wedding, and looking back over Becky's life. I couldn't help thinking of a tiny baby on a changing table, of a little girl in a flower-patterned dress running around the garden of my

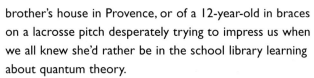

brother's house in Provence, or of a 12-year-old in braces on a lacrosse pitch desperately trying to impress us when we all knew she'd rather be in the school library learning about quantum theory.

But although Becky has had a distinguished career – she was one of the youngest students ever to gain a PhD from her University (thanks no doubt to that trap-like mind of hers) – she has always worn her learning lightly.

She's not afraid to laugh at herself and relax over a drink, even if she did once spend an entire evening in the pub trying to explain to me the difference between the specific weight of a glass of red wine, and specific gravity. Or was it the other way round?

Anyway, we feel she may have met her match in Mark. He may not be particularly clued up about quantum theory, but he is bright and has a wonderful sense of humour, so when Becky tells him one of her jokes, he can not only understand it but laugh at it.

Actually, she did tell a good joke the other day: What's the difference between a PhD in maths and a large pizza? Answer: you can feed a family of four with a large pizza. A fact Eleanor and I have been finding out all these years. And now Mark: it's your turn!

So ladies and gentlemen, we'd like to propose…'

Sample speech 5
An unusual proposal

'First of all, can I say how happy Grace (*bride's mother*) and I are to have so many old friends here today. It is really wonderful to see you all on this special day.

It's also marvellous that our darling daughter Liz is getting married today. And she couldn't have chosen a nicer, more loving husband than Gavin – although I have to say that we haven't always seen him as perfect son-in-law material…

We first met Gavin about five years ago, when he and Liz were "just good friends", as they say. Certainly good enough friends to turn up at our house on a Saturday night saying, when Grace opened the door, "I'm a friend of Liz's. Where can I be sick?"

We always thought of Gavin as rather similar to Liz's pet spaniel Sammie – amiable, friendly and not very good at keeping down his food. But a son-in-law? Not likely!

And we have to say that the way in which he went about getting Liz to marry him was not exactly "by the book". I hope I'm not treading on the best man's toes if I tell you the story of how he proposed. Some of you will have heard this story before, and I apologise to you. Some of you will know about it because you were there.

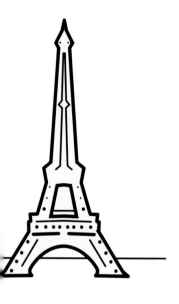

Yes, there were witnesses. Several, in fact.

Most men who are planning to propose to their future wives choose a romantic setting – the deck of a cruise liner, the hillside overlooking a Tuscan villa or the Eiffel Tower. Not for Gavin – he chose the bar at Garside Rugby Club.

And most men choose a moment when the two of them are alone. Not Gavin. By most credible accounts, there were between 40 and 50 people there. Even though it was two in the morning.

And finally, most grooms-to-be feel the need for a quick drink to stiffen the sinews and gird up the loins. Nothing wrong with that. But Gavin chose the night of the Rugby Club ball and had been – how shall I put it? – *celebrating* the fact that the team that he captained had just been relegated for the third year in succession. He wasn't exactly *compos mentis*. In fact, rumour has it that the conversation went like this:

Gavin (*put-on drunken voice*): "Darling, it's time to go home and go to bed."

Liz: "Yes, OK dear."

Gavin: "And another thing." (*Pause.*) "Will you carry me?"

A couple of weeks later the misunderstanding was sorted out. It happened at our house, actually, when Gavin felt the need to get his future father-in-law's blessing. Which, after recovering from the shock, I readily gave. It was when Liz came back from a shopping trip, and Grace and I congratulated her warmly, that we discovered that she had no idea he had actually proposed to her!

Today, though, Gavin seems to have behaved impeccably. And of course sons-in-law have an immeasurable advantage: the fact that they love your daughter and find her the most beautiful girl in the world puts them up several notches in your estimation.

And so it is with great pleasure that we welcome Gavin to our family. And it is also with great pleasure that I propose...'

Sample speech 6

Losing a daughter…

'Ladies and gentlemen, first let me say how fantastic it is to see you all today.

I am very, *very* happy to be standing in front of you today, because it's absolutely wonderful to see our beautiful daughter Marion looking so ecstatic. Marion, we are so very proud of you and hope that you and Jon will be as happy as Louise and I have been for all these years.

Many of you will know that until just a few months ago, Marion had been living at home with Louise and me. When Marion finished university, we imagined that she would do what all the other young women of her generation seemed to do, which was to leave the nest as fast as she could.

So it was rather a surprise, but a great pleasure as well, that Marion showed absolutely no interest in that sort of thing. "No, daddy," she said to me one day, "I'm perfectly happy at home with you and mum, and if I was living with a husband, I wouldn't be able to stay in the bathroom so long in the mornings."

Of course, as the years went by, we broached the subject occasionally. These attempts were met with a frosty look, or, at best, some kind of remark such as "*When* I meet the perfect man, daddy, I'll let you know" – in rather the same tone as you might say "When pigs fly…"

There *were* boyfriends. Well, perhaps "boyfriends" is putting it a bit strongly. There were men who turned up at our house and asked for Marion. We weren't actually asked to man the barricades against them, but they often went away with a flea in their ear. Marion, as many of you will know, was so deeply involved in her work at the Royal Institute by then that she didn't have time for men. Or so she said…

In fact, I think that in our heart of hearts, we thought that maybe Marion wasn't the marrying kind. That was fine by us – we loved having her around (even if it meant less time for us in the bathroom). But then, about eight months ago, Marion announced she was going out in the evening and not to a conference or a lecture, but on… a date. Wow!

This produced mixed feelings. The prospect of cutting down from three to two in a household would be a big shock. On the other hand, we were immensely pleased for Marion, and when we met Jon – about three hours later, as it turned out – we were sure that she had met a man who would truly love her. And while young love is all the rage, mature love may be the best of all.

So, we welcome Jon into our family with open arms. All we say to him is: just make sure you buy a house with two bathrooms!'

Sample speech 7
Childhood sweethearts

'Treasured friends, dearest family – the happy couple.
Welcome and thank you for joining us in what is proving
to be the most wonderful and happiest day of my life.
Apart from my own wedding day, of course.

Seeing my darling daughter Michelle marry her
childhood sweetheart, Nathan, has been a magical
experience – one I will never forget. I'm so proud of you,
darling. And proud of you, too – son.

Before I get to the toasts – one of which it is my great
pleasure to propose today – and before I begin to work
through a long list of thank-yous to an army of people who
have helped make today so special – I'd like to take a
moment to say a few words about my new son-in-law.
And before he gets too anxious, I can tell him it's
all good. Well, most of it anyway.

Nathan is my first son-in-law and
so, to gauge what I could fairly expect
from him in terms of his qualities and
attributes, I turned to my esteemed
friends at the golf club, all of whom have
their own sons-in-law. Thanks, lads, for all
your insight and wisdom.

So what did my friends say I could expect from Nathan as my son-in-law? What noble qualities and manly attributes could I, the patriarch of the family, expect from this newest male addition? Their answers were… enlightening. And, to help me remember them, I've made a mnemonic of them, which spells out N-A-T-H-A-N.

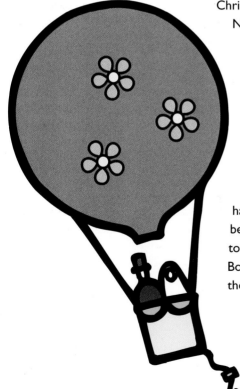

N for Nathan. The first quality I should expect, my mates tell me, is Neutrality. In any situation, especially a family dispute, your son-in-law should always take a non-confrontational stance. A good idea in principle, but when the debate starts in August about where we're all spending Christmas — as it does every year — I'll be impressed if Nathan stays neutral. Just don't mention going away skiing, son… for all our sakes.

A is for the next invaluable quality — Ambition. Not that I'm that competitive, but if you don't want to beat my highest score snooker break — of 26, I might add — then you're not likely to get on in our household. Mind you, I wouldn't want him to actually beat it, of course…

Next comes T for Tirelessness. You've got to have stamina in this family. Games of Scrabble have been known to last several days. Pat often treats us to a 12-hour eat-athon on special occasions, and the Boxing Day walk to the Fox and Hounds is not for the faint-hearted.

Then we have H for Honesty. When Nathan asked for Michelle's hand in marriage, and I looked into his eyes and asked if he'd always take care of her, I could tell he was being honest when he said, "I promise I'll try, with all my heart, never to let her down." I respect that and know, in my heart, you'll do as you promised. Of course, I won't mention the fact that you denied opening my 1971 Montrachet last Christmas and then putting it in the punch, despite the bottle turning up in the back of your car two days later. Not today, anyway…

Next, another A – for Alacrity. To get on in our family, you need to be eager and ready to get stuck in. And after I saw you in fancy dress at last summer's barn dance, I know you have this quality in spades. Shame your costume let you down at the last minute – I'll never forget the look on Pat's face when your chaps rode up so unfortunately.

Last, but by no means least, is N for Nobility – in the truest sense of the word. Since I've known you, Nathan, you've always been someone with exemplary manners and a keen sense of duty. You're an honourable man who obviously loves his family and my daughter, and you have earned the love of me and my family too.

Nathan, you're a credit to your mum and dad and I'm glad and proud to call you my son-in-law. And so, ladies and gentlemen: to the happy couple!'

Sample speech 8
Modern girl

'Ladies and gentlemen, family and friends of both bride and groom, and all who have made the effort to be here on this wonderful day, I'd like to take this opportunity to thank you and acknowledge all those who have helped in the preparation and celebration of today's glorious event: the union of my lovely daughter Hayley and my fine new son-in-law, Malcolm, as they commence a life in partnership.

I now have the pleasure and privilege of expressing a few thoughts about my wonderful little girl.

I stand before you a twenty-first-century man – thanks to Hayley. Her passion for the new technologies of the last 25 years has brought me, at times kicking and screaming, into the modern age.

Even as a child, Hayley had a boundless enthusiasm for gadgets and gizmos. When she was nine she insisted on having a mobile phone. This was at the time when they looked like bricks and cost a thousand pounds. As always, I relented, sort of. It looked like a mobile, even sounded like one, but was only a toy one.

Over the past decade or so, Hayley must have got through hundreds of mobile phones, but has always insisted that her dad should share in the advances of telecoms. Until my daughter taught me otherwise, I thought that "Bluetooth" was something you got from eating too much ice cream. Thanks to Hayley, I now send numerous texts each month, and I always get a thrill from the daily "love you dad" with which Hayley ends her texts to me.

Then there's the internet. Be it emails or instant messaging, surfing the web or Facebook, my dear daughter has always revelled in the potentials of cyberspace and has urged me to get acquainted with the web too. At first I resisted, especially as I had to foot the hefty bills from something called "Topshop.co.uk". But one day Hayley sat me down and logged me on to something called "Itunes". From that glorious moment on, when I discovered I could download my favourite songs from the Kinks and the Small Faces, I was a believer!

Then there were the computer games. I thought I was a thoroughly modern dad when I bought Hayley Kerplunk. How wrong was I! As soon as the Sega Mega Drive appeared, all she wanted to play was "Sonic the Hedgehog". Through the telly! I can't tell you the number of programmes my wife and I sacrificed in order for Hayley and her friends to be Lara Croft or Spyro the Dragon. For those of you who haven't the faintest idea what I'm talking about, pretend you do… it gives your age away.

But as always, it was Hayley's firm but loving insistence that I play these games with her which brought me to see their wonder: a chance to be silly and share laughter together. And when I opened a birthday present from her with the wondrous title, "Fifa World Cup '98", I was well and truly hooked.

I now see and appreciate Hayley's love of all these technologies for what it really is – a small part of her desire to make life easier, to inject more fun and laughter into all our lives and to bring families and friends closer. Today, however, I need rely on no gizmo or gadget to tell you all how proud I am of you, my darling girl, how delighted I am that you and Malcolm have found each other, and how very much your mother and I love and adore you.

And now, ladies and gentlemen, please be upstanding. I give you… the bride and groom.'

Sample speech 9
The baby of the family

'Ladies and gentlemen, I'd like to take this opportunity to thank you all for being here. Whether you've come from far or near, you are all very welcome guests on this happy day – the marriage of our wonderful daughter Jane to our brand-new and equally wonderful son-in-law David. My wife and I particularly want to thank Kay and Graham, David's parents, for their kind generosity and enormous help with planning today's very special event.

As many of you will know, Jane is the youngest of our six children. It isn't easy being the baby of the family, and over the years it has presented her with as many trials and tribulations as it has blessings. So today, as she embarks on a life in partnership with David, I thought it apt to underline her many wonderful qualities by summarizing her – at times turbulent – journey from kid sister to beautiful bride.

A common assumption about youngest members of a big brood is that they're spoilt rotten. Not so in our Jane's case. The first thing she learnt from being the youngest of six was humility. From the constant character-forming ribbing by her elder siblings to the endless ill-fitting hand-me-downs, Jane has had to find her feet walking a well-worn trail left by her flamboyant and raucous older siblings.

As a toddler, Jane had to get used to her brothers and sisters' greedy mealtime mantra: "One spoon of tasty chocolate pudding for you, Jane… and three spoons for me." The poor starved mite!

Jane's early attempts at a sartorial style of her own, be it school uniforms or brownie outfits, were met with guffaws and derision. Her first attempt at make-up, aged 12, brought more cackles as well as unkind comparisons to a multicoloured panda bear or a survivor of an explosion at a lipstick factory. Yet my darling girl met all such ignominies with a fortitude and grace that not only earned her the love of her elders, but their respect too.

Her teens were perhaps the greatest test of her character. Most school holidays were spent visiting family members who'd flown the nest. After every jaunt to a halls of residence or scuzzy London flat-share, Jane would return home with radical ideas.

Her eight o'clock bedtime would be greeted with the revolutionary cry: "If I were with my sisters, we'd just be going out now." And of her school friends whose birthday parties consisted of Pass the Parcel she'd yawn and say: "I find them all *so* passé!" (That Jane had no idea what "passé" meant never got in the way.)

Yet her teething truculence always went hand-in-hand with good-natured assurances that though she thought her mum and me "outdated fascists", she loved us just the same.

So today, with a happy heart, I wish you every blessing, my darling daughter. For as much as your family has taught you, so you, in return, have taught us. Your humility, your big heart and your eagerness to do the best you can, no matter how difficult, stand you in good stead for a wonderful and fulfilling life.

Take care of her David, she's a treasure. And don't let her siblings convince you otherwise.

Ladies and gentlemen, I give you the bride and groom…'

Toasts

The father of the bride traditionally toasts the bride and groom at the end of his speech.

A traditional approach

'Today is all about two people and their decision to spend the rest of their lives together. We wish them good luck and great joy, today and always. So please stand and raise your glasses with me… To the happy couple!'

'I end my speech today by thanking you all for joining us to celebrate the wedding of Annabel and Ben. It's been a wonderful day so far and we hope this will be the beginning of a wonderful life together for them. Please join me in wishing them all the best… To Annabel and Ben!'

Bit of banter

'Before we raise our glasses, John, I'd like you to take Diana's hand and place your own over it. Now remember and cherish this special moment, because believe me, if I know my daughter, this is the last time you'll have the upper hand… To Diana and John!'

Quick quip

'**Apparently, my wife tells me, I'm now supposed to make toast. Good grief! Haven't you all eaten enough already?**'

'Ah, right, I see, I'm supposed to make a toast. Well, then, please stand and raise your glasses quickly before I mess anything else up and join with me in wishing John and Emma every happiness... To the bride and groom!'

Getting sentimental

'**It's said that when children find true love, parents find true joy – and true joy is what I am feeling today. As a father, whatever else I may have wanted for my children, my abiding wish has always been for them to find relationships in which they can be truly happy. I know Katie has found this with Daniel. Katie, as everyone knows, is the apple of my eye. So for me to say that I have gained a wonderful son-in-law is the greatest compliment that I can give. Ladies and gentlemen, I would like you to join me in drinking a toast to the happy couple. Please be upstanding and raise your glasses to Katie and Daniel.**'

Index

About confetti.co.uk

Confetti.co.uk, founded in 1999, is the leading destination for brides- and grooms-to-be. Every month over 500,000 people visit www.confetti.co.uk to help them plan their weddings and special occasions. Here is a quick guide to our website

Weddings The wedding channel is packed full of advice and ideas to make your day more special and your planning less stressful. Our personalized planning tools will ensure you won't forget a thing.

Celebrations Checklists, advice and ideas for every party and celebration.

Fashion and beauty View hundreds of wedding, bridesmaid and party dresses and accessories. Get expert advice on how to look and feel good.

Travel Search for the most idyllic destinations for your honeymoon, wedding abroad or romantic breaks. Get fun ideas for hen and stag weekends.

Suppliers Thousands of suppliers to choose from including venues, gift lists companies, cake makers, florists and bridal retailers.

Café Talk to other brides and grooms and get ideas from our real life weddings section. Ask Aunt Betti, our agony aunt, for advice.

Shop All your wedding and party essentials in one place. The ranges include planning essentials, books and CDs, personalised stationery for weddings and celebrations, create your own trims, ribbons and papers, table decorations, party products including hen and stag, memories and gifts. If you'd like to do your shopping in person or view all the ranges before buying online, please visit the confetti stores.

Online

• Shop online 24 hours a day 7 days a week, use quick searches by department, product code or keyword, use the online order tracking facility and view brand new products as soon as they come out.

• Shop by phone on 0870 840 6060 Monday to Friday between 9 am and 5 pm.

• Shop by post by sending a completed order form to Confetti, Freepost NEA9292, Carr Lane, Low Moor, Bradford, BD12 0BR or fax on 01274 805 741.

By phone/freepost

Request your free copy of our catalogue online at www.confetti.co.uk or call 0870 840 6060

In store

London – 80 Tottenham Court Road, London, W1T 4TE

Leeds – The Light, The Headrow, Leeds, LS1 8TL

Birmingham – 43 Temple Street, Birmingham B2 5DP

Glasgow – 15–17 Queen Street, Glasgow, G1 3ED

Reading – 159 Friar Street, Reading, RG1 1HE

Executive Editor **Katy Denny**
Editor **Fiona Robertson**
Executive Art Editor **Joanna MacGregor**
Design **'OMEDESIGN**
Production Manager **Ian Paton**